D0005442

Steve McMichael's
Tales from the

BEARS SIDELINE

Steve McMichael
with Phil Arvia

Sports Publishing L.L.C.
www.SportsPublishingLLC.com

Director of production: Susan M. Moyer
Acquisitions editor: Scott Musgrave
Project manager: Kathryn R. Holleman
Developmental editor: Dean Miller
Dust jacket designer and imaging: Heidi Norsen
Copy editor: Cynthia L. McNew
Marketing manager: Mike Hagan

ISBN: 1-58261-800-3

Printed in the United States of America.

Sports Publishing L.L.C.
www.SportsPublishingLLC.com

CONTENTS

FOREWORD

When I first came to the Bears as head coach, my wife and I went out to dinner at a place in Lake Forest on a Friday night. We had a game coming on Sunday.

I'd never been to this place, but she wanted to go, so we went. We got seated at the restaurant, and a couple minutes later the waitress came back and said, "A couple of your players would like to buy you and your wife a drink."

I said, "OK," and asked, "Where are they?" She said, "Out in the bar."

So I went out to the bar, and there was Steve McMichael, Dan Hampton and Mike Hartenstine—three of my key players—doing shots of tequila. What could I do?

I said, "I'll see you at practice tomorrow morning." They were all there and they were ready to go.

I never tried to treat those guys like kids. They weren't kids; they were adults, they were men, men who went out and busted their ass. So what am I going to do, get on them because they had a couple beers or whatever?

What can you say? That's the way that group of guys was. They were throwbacks to the old years I had with the Bears as a player. We played hard, we ran hard and we took our chances. That's what I liked about them.

That's what I liked about Steve McMichael.

Steve's a throwback to the old ballplayers. What you see is what you get, whether you like it or not. He's the real deal. I always liked Steve, because he gave me everything he had on the field. He played like a warrior, and that's what I appreciate most about him.

Vince Lombardi said you'd never have a great player until you get one who knows how to play the game not only with his head, but also with his heart. Steve knew both. When I looked at him, I looked at a guy for whom things didn't come easy, but his work ethic was second to nobody on the football team.

When he went on the field, I don't think he ever got the recognition he deserved because we had a lot of good people on our defense—but our defense would not have been nearly as good without Steve McMichael, believe me. He made everybody else's job a little easier with the way he played the game.

When we had Steve and William Perry playing the tackles, and Dan Hampton, it was as good a group of guys as you could ask for, really. Then you bring Richard Dent on the outside, and of course we had great linebackers with Mike Singletary, Wilber Marshall and Otis Wilson. Add in the secondary led by Gary Fencik, and it was just a great defense.

I think Steve was an integral part of that defense in every way. When you look at our stats and find out how many pressures he had on the quarterback, how many knock downs—he didn't always get the sack, but I know he was there chasing him into somebody else's arms.

He doesn't try to impress anybody with the fact that he is smart, that he knows what he's doing. Steve can sense things, he can feel things out, he can anticipate things on defense.

He wants to give the image that he's the guy digging the ditch, that he's the hard worker. Nobody's ever going to accuse him of being Phi Beta Kappa, yet he's very smart about the way he played the game of football—and he had to be, because our defense demanded players recognize formations and adjust.

A lot of what Buddy Ryan did, what we did, was confusing the offense. If they can't recognize, they can't block. If you're going to screw up their blocking assignments, there's nobody for them to block, they're not going to do a good job. We did that, and we had athletic ability. You can play any defense, but if you don't have the athletes to do it, it's not going to work. We had the athletes to do it, and that's what made it so much fun.

Of course, there's no question Steve had a lot of fun. Very few people had more fun than Steve McMichael, but that's OK. There's a time to work and a time to play, when it was time to work and practice, he did that, and when it was time to have fun, he did that. I never had a problem with guys like that.

Steve never wanted to give the impression that he did all the right things, but he did a lot of the right things, believe me.

His honesty—you may not like what he says, but he's going to say it. He doesn't pull any punches.

I knew I could count on Steve. On that football team, I was lucky in the sense that there wasn't anybody, really, whom I couldn't count on. They were all guys that kept the other guys in line. Steve, though, was really in that core group of players that controlled the other players—and you do that basically through example.

The example Steve set on and off the field, was good. He was one of the best in practice. He practiced hard. He was a guy who practiced to get better.

Also, I think he was a role model for other guys. Not that he did everything in the world right, but he certainly did it at a full-speed pace.

Steve was small for a defensive tackle even then, but he was strong—exceptionally strong. As far as his upper body went, he was as strong as anybody we had on the football team. He spent a lot of time in the weight room.

When I first got there, I realized he was a player. I didn't have a lot of decisions when I looked at some of the other guys we had. Some of the other guys had bigger reputations than Steve, yet when I watched Steve play I liked what I saw. I liked the way he practiced; I like the way he worked. He just went about his job as a man.

Steve was a lot like I was when I played. He liked to raise a little hell, and on occasion I did that myself.

What I looked for from Steve is what I had as a player. I played hard, I didn't want to get beat by anybody, I didn't want to take a back seat to anybody. I think that's the way Steve played the game.

MIKE DITKA

ACKNOWLEDGMENTS

The authors would like to thank Scott Hagel and the Chicago Bears for their assistance; the *Daily Southtown* for help with research and photos; and Misty McMichael for the snacks—even the caviar.

Chapter 1

THE EARLY YEARS

DOME, SWEET DOME

Before I was a football player, I was a jumper. I liked to jump off of things. I still have a scar under my chin from tying a towel around my neck and jumping off the sewing machine to see if I could fly.

Now these are just flashes I can remember. You ought to remember I've used my head for a living, and I've killed a lot of brain cells.

My natural father left when I was two. After he left, my mom, Betty, was living and working up in Pasadena, a suburb that's now part of Houston, and met the man I consider my real father, E.V. McMichael. He never liked his natural name, didn't cotton to Eurie, Eurie Vance, so he just had folks call him E.V. His nickname was Mac, and that's what I called him to the day he was killed.

Anyway, they moved to a house in Pasadena, just down from the Astrodome. I was about four years old. I crawled up on the house—got a ladder, put it on the side of the roof and crawled up it—with an umbrella to see if I could float down.

But when I got up there, I saw they were putting up the big girders for the Astrodome. They were just starting to build it. I asked, "What is that?" They said, "They're building a football stadium."

That was my first recollection that there was such a thing as football.

EVERYBODY'S ALL-STATER

When I was five years old, Mac got a job in the oil fields in Freer, Texas, so we all moved down there—me, Mom, Mac, my older brother Richard and my two new little sisters, Kathy and Sharon. Freer had a Class 2A school, 2,800 people in the whole town. And I say there was an oil field—*was*. Mac eventually sucked it dry.

They didn't have peewee football. Had to wait until the seventh grade, junior high, until I could put pads on.

I was playing running back. In seventh grade, our quarterback had such a weak arm, he'd pitch the ball and I would throw it. Never got under center, though. I think quarterback was the only position I never played.

I have a reel of our last football team, and man, I never came off the field. I kicked, I was the tight end on offense, I played middle linebacker. I'm one of the few guys in America who, in my senior year, made All-State three ways, and I'm in the Texas High School Hall of Fame for football.

Hell, my senior year, I had six letters—football, basketball, baseball, track, tennis and golf. Track, I threw the shotput and discus. Tennis, I was the only guy in town who played the singles. There were a couple of doubles players and I practiced with them. It was usually just to get on the coed bus. You'd go to the tennis meet and get beat, but then it's all day with the girls.

Other bus rides weren't so much fun.

Football down in Texas, baby, there's a fever about it. We only lost one regular-season game my whole high school career, so there was some animosity. We'd know to get on the floor of the bus, because there were going to be rocks thrown in the windows leaving town.

An early action shot of me on the gridiron.

Worse, playing offense for the Freer Buckaroos, you were a marked man. The little towns in the district we were from, we were like archenemies. One of the teams, San Diego, it was the closest town to us, about 30 miles away—I told you it was in the middle of the oil fields.

Our quarterback was Jim Acker, who ended up playing pro baseball for about 15 years, and I played football at the University of Texas with his older brother, Bill. The San Diego Vaqueros were the team that got Jim's knee—and they were going after it. They were going after mine, too.

It was my senior year; both towns were at the game. Everybody saw them going after our knees, and when they got him, both stands emptied. There was the big thing in the middle of the field, both teams, the people from town, all fighting. I knew who was responsible for it, so I started heading for the head coach. Well, he saw me coming and hauled ass down the sideline.

I still have a calcium deposit on my right leg from playing fullback—a deep hematoma. Going through the line, one kid grabbed my thigh pad trying to tackle me and moved it over. The next one, boom, into my thigh.

Still have that calcium deposit. That kind of influenced my decision on college. I wanted to be the one giving the hematoma.

TO READ OR TO THE REDS?

I really liked playing baseball more than football, to tell you the truth. I was the catcher on the baseball team at Freer, and I was better at baseball than football.

The Cincinnati Reds and the St. Louis Cardinals came to see me, but my parents wanted me to go to college and get a

With my parents Betty and E.V. McMichael behind me, I signed to play at the University of Texas. (Photo by Alice Echo—News Journal)

degree. When they came to see me, I had already signed to play college football.

SAYING NO TO A BEAR

I had about 75 recruiting letters of intent from major colleges. Bear Bryant, the legend at Alabama, called me on the phone. My high school team ran the veer, just two backs. I was the tight end in that. In the wishbone, I was the fullback.

Bear told me, "I'll make you an All-American at tight end." I told him, "Bear, I want to be the hitter, not the hittee." It was that hematoma talking.

Darrell Royal, who was at Texas, told me, "We're going to play you at defensive end." Defensive end was really more like an outside linebacker. Back then, with the option, it was like a linebacker playing contain.

So I went to Texas.

It broke E.V.'s heart, because he was a cajun from Louisiana and he wanted me to go to LSU. But Texas was the bright, shining star where I was from. Darrell Royal was there, Earl Campbell was there, and my buddy from Freer, Bill Acker, was already there. He ended up calling us the Fear from Freer.

The last two years we ended up starting right beside each other, the two defensive tackles. That's pretty amazing, a 2A school having two defensive tackles at the University of Texas.

So Darrell Royal tells me he's going to play me on defense. What do you think happens the first day, right out of the box, at practice? The coach says, "Uh, Steve, are you a team player? Because we need you to play tight end."

I loved the guy. Everybody who knows him loves him. It's like what everybody says when they meet a president, "Man, he made me feel like I was the only one in the room." He had that. That's why he had good teams. People come to play for people like that.

A few games later, one of Earl Campbell's twin brothers, Tim, was playing defensive end and he got hurt. Then it's, "OK, Steve, we want you to play defensive end now." So I moved over there.

ON THE JOB

There was a change in college. I realized right away, when I first stepped on the campus, that football was different. In high school, it was a game. At the University of Texas, it was a business—that football factory thing. But I didn't want to be a factory worker. My degree plan was pre-dentistry.

At every stage of my career—it happened in high school, happened in college, happened in New England when I got to the pros—I was told that I'd never be successful on the next level.

So I had a plan.

That whole area down there, where I'm from, Duvall County, no dentists. I'd have had all the business.

I've always had a plan. Until somebody fucks with me. Then I get immediate.

BECOMING IMMEDIATE

The first game they started me my freshman year was at Texas Tech, Lubbock. That's the night Mac was killed.

He'd been to all my games. There was a guy down in Freer who had a private plane and he offered to fly Mac to the game that weekend, but for some reason Mac said no.

My mother didn't call me. She sent my father's foreman, who worked under him in the oil fields, and Jim Acker, my old quarterback. They both came up to Austin to get me, knocked on my door the next morning, and told me.

I don't want to get into what happened, but the bottom line is, he's gone. What came out of that, for me, as it pertained to my football playing, it was like a rage. An immediate rage. Here, something was taken from me, and I was playing a game that was all about the offense wanting to take.

I became immediate.

What I mean is, when the shit hits the fan in a street fight, you've got two choices looking at the person in front of you. One is to whip his ass. The other is to make allowances and walk away.

After that happened, I wasn't making any allowances.

LIKE A MOTH TO A FLAME

Another thing changed. I became a wild child. After what happened, in my mind, you better grab life by the throat because it can be taken from you real fast, before you want it to be over. That's when I started having an affinity for the neon lights. Before, I was the big-headed jock. All I did was go to school and play sports.

Down in Freer, everybody knows where you are every minute of the day. Even when you've got a girl out, they know where your car is, they know where it's passed by. E.V. McMichael wouldn't have put up with me being a wild child. I had a curfew, and at all times my mother was about enforcing the curfew. But in college, as a moth to flame, old Mongo was to the neon lights—even before they started calling me Mongo.

Actually, I was a bouncer for a time, in a strip club. You know how every college kid has a side job for a little extra money? Mine was bouncing. I'm telling you, it was a dream job. I've always been a bully's bully. But don't take that to mean I was the best bully. I bullied the bullies. Even in elementary school, I'd see a bigger kid bullying a smaller one, and I'd take up for the little kid.

Or the stripper.

They'd come into the club from time to time beat up, and most of the time it would be the man they were living with doing the beating.

I'd say, "Just tell me who he is when he comes here to pick you up tonight." There was a side exit door, and I'd go wait for them in the dark.

Those girls never got hit again.

Back when I was immediate, I used to do that in bars with total strangers.

A guy would be dominating a woman, and I'd step in front of him. My phrase was, "Son, I'm going to teach you what it's like to get out of your weight class."

There were two avenues he could take. He could stand there and be apologetic; then allowances were made. If he was a smartass, I'd begin the process of beating him down.

But when I'd get him beat down, who do you think jumped on my back the majority of the time? The woman. I'd tell 'em, "That's why he's beating your ass."

OVERLOOKED, UNDERAPPRECIATED

I've always sucked hind tit when it comes to awards. Most of those college All-Star games, the MVP gets the keys to a car. Well, at the Hula Bowl my senior year, I was told I was MVP before the game was over, so I'm thinking, "Man, I'm getting a new car."

I knew I was the best defensive player on the field. We ended up losing the game, but the opposing coach was Bo Schembechler. They interviewed him on the sideline and he said, "If it wasn't for McMichael, we'd be killing these guys."

At the end of the game, I walked out there on the field with the governor of Hawaii, and he handed me a wooden monkey bowl. For some reason, that's what they called it—a wooden bowl with a little plaque on it.

It was just something else to fuel me, like my sophomore year at college.

Playing with Earl Campbell, we were 11-0 going to the Cotton Bowl. Every year before that, both teams that went to the game got a Rolex commemorative Cotton Bowl watch.

We got a Seiko.

Another thing that happened that sophomore year, I played against the pox on my career for the rest of my football life—Joe Montana. He beat the hell out of us—and me in particular. Then he did it in pro football. But I consider him the best quarterback of all time.

Why me in particular? I was there, and it's all about me, isn't it?

The bowl is nice and all, but where's my car?

That's the immediate I'm talking about. What about me? Why is this happening to me?

HONEST TO A FAULT

In the three years I played defensive tackle—my sophomore year they moved me to tackle because I was in the weight room and getting a little bigger—I had 358 tackles and 30 sacks. That's why I made All-America two times, my junior and senior year, and All-Conference three times.

Actually, my college defensive line coach, Mike Parker, is a big reason for all of those honors and my pro career. He's the one who taught me the technique that helped make me a pro.

Anyway, my sophomore spring, just like in Freer, I was picked out for injury—and this time my own roommate did it to me on purpose.

I was going through the Texas offense like shit through a goose, and my roommate, the starting center, got fed up with it. He set me up. The guard hit me high and he dove across the back of my legs.

Tore a bucket-handle tear in my meniscus, my cartilage.

I didn't get it operated on. Played my junior and senior year with it. Nobody knew. After my senior year, I went to the Hula Bowl—shoot, I wanted to go to Hawaii. I scheduled an operation before going into pro ball.

Pro teams were coming down there scouting. The Steelers' Chuck Knoll actually came to Texas, working me out as Mike Webster's replacement snapping the ball.

I had a chance to go in the first round until I started telling all these people, "You know, I have a hurt knee and I'm getting it operated on."

Boom. Third round.

Still, it worked out OK. I ended up being the defensive MVP of the game—14 tackles, a sack—and that's the main reason the Bears brought me to Chicago. The general manager at the time, Jim Finks, told me, "The way you played in the Hula Bowl is the reason we're giving you a chance, kid."

Of course, that was almost two years later.

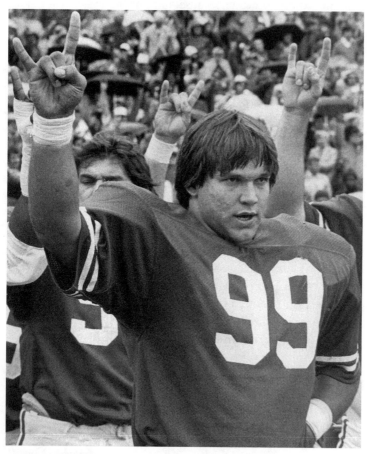

Hook 'em, Horns!

Chapter 2

THE CRIMINAL ELEMENT

BIG MONEY

The New England Patriots ended up taking me in the third round of the 1980 draft—No. 72 overall.

For a third-round defensive tackle, I got the most money ever paid at the time—a $45,000 signing bonus and a three-year contract, $45,000, $55,000 and $75,000. Big money, ain't it?

I bought a Cadillac, and I bought my mother one, too. Hers was a new Fleetwood Brougham, and mine was a used Coupe de Ville.

NEW ENGLAND, OLD STORY

I was still immediate. The way I was in a rage in practice, I think those coaches up in New England took it for arrogance, a nega-

My college career ended with me as a Bob Hope All-American and a third-round draft pick.

tive they didn't want on their team. In a way, I guess I never really was on their team. But I tried.

As soon as I stepped on the field, who was there? John "Hog" Hannah. He was just on the cover of *Sports Illustrated,* "The Best Offensive Lineman of All Time." First thing out of the box, there was a drill called the nutcracker—my kind of game, brother.

It's a one-on-one confrontation with a running back coming through, like an offensive play is being run at you. Single-team block, you against him, and if the running back gets through, he wins. If you get rid of him and tackle the running back, you win. They put the little dummy bags about five yards apart—that's a gap.

When it starts out, there's a line and you wait your turn to go. Rookies are in the back. John Hannah's at the front. When he walked up to get in between the bags, I walked up to the front and told the veteran, Tony "Mack the Sack" McGee, "Excuse me, Mack the Sack, I think it's my turn."

He was only too happy to let me go. The coaches, they're like, "This little smartass, arrogant kid."

I got up there, stuffed him and made the tackle. He got up and said, "You embarrassed me that time, kid."

The next time up, Hannah taught me that pro football is not going to be fair. He taught me it wasn't going to measure up to the rulebook. I mean, you know holding, clipping, it goes on all the time. But the punching... He came off the ball with an uppercut to my gut with one of his fists. I was trying to hit his shoulder pads with my hands—and you know, that leaves your gut open, baby. He actually lifted my feet off the ground with this uppercut, and the running back went through. I told him, "Thanks. Thanks for the lesson."

When they released me, John was one of the guys who came down when I was cleaning out my locker and said, "Don't listen to them, kid. You've got a pro football career. They made a mistake releasing you."

Those guys aren't fake. The guys who are considered the greatest didn't win a popularity contest. They're good. They know what's going on and how to play the game.

STANDING PAT

New England is like any other NFL team. They procrastinate. They don't want to admit their mistakes. Look at the Bears with Cade McNown.

But they weren't going to play me. I never got on the field my rookie year. They actually put me on injured reserve, saying I had a back injury, just so they wouldn't have to release me. I stuck around to practice against the offense, at least until camp was almost over in '81.

They've got a name for it in football—"The Turk." They send a guy down there to say, "The head coach wants to see you, and bring your playbook."

They had a name for me, too. The head coach, Ron Erhardt, told me one of the reasons they were releasing me was that "we believe you're part of the criminal element in the league."

They knew I was running around, they'd have nosy rat fans writing in saying, "I've seen this guy running around all hours of the night."

Back in Boston in those days, the Combat Zone was still open. You better believe there were some practices they knew I didn't have any sleep before. It's that area like any city has, the bar row, like Rush Street in Chicago. Because it was called the Combat Zone is why it was eventually shut down. But that's what drew me—the Combat Zone? That sounds pretty interesting.

So there was that, plus the fact that this immediate fucker was fighting in practice all the time. A guy'd hold me, I'd fire up. Nothing really. Even most street fights don't last a minute.

Anyway, I knew what they meant. The criminal element. I was thinking, "Time to go to work."

I broke in with the Patriots before I was identified as part of "the criminal element."

THE HALAS HAUL

I was still in New England the next day. The Bears called me on the phone; they wanted to give me a tryout. That's another thing New England did—it was the end of camp, the year was fixing to start, there were no openings.

The Bears wanted to give me a tryout to be the backup center behind Dan Neal. They had Jay Hilgenberg, but he was a free agent that year and he didn't know his way around how to play center in pro football. Me and Dan Hampton eventually taught him, though.

So the Bears asked, "When can you be here?" I told them, "Tomorrow morning." I got into Chicago late that night, in my Cadillac. That's just over 1,000 miles, Boston to Lake Forest.

The next morning, they tried me out at center. What they were really looking for was a center who could deep-snap, and I wasn't that. When they found out I couldn't do that, they sent me home. A "Don't call us, we'll call you" deal.

So in a couple of days, two teams cut me, and I drove back to Austin.

HULA OR HALAS?

In October, the Bears called me back. One of the guys I played college ball with, Brad Shearer, was a backup defensive tackle for the Bears. But he had a bad knee, and every time the cold weather would hit the couple years he was there, he was no use to them. Seven weeks into the season, he hurt his knee again, and that was the end of his career.

Jim Finks called me up and said, "Because of the way you played in the Hula Bowl, and the fact that we need a backup defensive tackle, we're going to give you a contract."

Yeah, Finks called me, but really I think it was George Halas who wanted me on that team. You know the collusion these owners are in, and I was the black sheep in the NFL. The Sullivans owned the Patriots at the time, and if I was the criminal element to them, you don't think they put the word out?

But Halas, he was all about violence. The way he played football, it wasn't a patty-cake. How do you think they got the moniker "Monsters of the Midway?" It was because everybody knew they played against those fuckers the next day.

BUDDY AND THE DOG

Up to the point the Bears called me, in my mind, when the season was over, I was going to go try out somewhere. So I was staying in shape. I was jogging and lifting in my spare time, but it wasn't my job any more—my job was selling tax shelters, but that's another story.

Old Buddy Ryan, the mean old sergeant he was, a sarcastic guy—my kind of guy, really, and he found that out—he disrespected players until they proved something to him. He'd call you by your number, "Hey 76."

After a while he started calling me "Tex," so I knew I'd impressed him.

But in that first practice, I was definitely "76." Before the practice, he asked me, "You been working out?" I said, "Yeah, I got a big black Great Dane, and me and him been jogging."

They worked my ass off in practice. I was taking every rep, especially since Alan Page was there, the last year of his career, and he never practiced.

Even the best shape I've ever been in, if I take every rep in practice, I'm going to be gassed. So I was gassed after practice.

Buddy Ryan walks past me going into the locker room. You know what he says?

"Shit, 76, we shoulda hired the dog."

BAD NEWS BEARS

The first game after that practice that week, we played *Monday Night Football* against the Detroit Lions, and they weren't that good a team, either.

They ended up killing us, 48-17, and I didn't get to step on the field that night. So the game was over, and I ain't even played in this game, against a bad team that killed my team. In my mind, we're the worst team in the league—and I can't even play for this fucker? I might as well go home.

But I didn't.

I still remember one of the defensive ends from the Detroit Lions, Bubba Baker, and he's going against our offensive lineman Dan Jiggetts. Baker was killing him so bad that Neill Armstrong, our coach, pulled him. The backup was going to do worse, but to be a smartass Bubba came by the sideline yelling, "Come on, Armstrong, put Jiggetts back in."

STAYING AND PLAYING ARE TWO DIFFERENT THINGS

In my youthful arrogance, I thought I was better than everybody.

That helps. Sometimes arrogance is a good thing in sports. Every good starting quarterback has got that confident arrogance—I'm better than everybody. The bad ones don't have it. McNown just acted like he did.

I wasn't really playing, just special teams. The tackles in front of me, Jim Osborne, who had a 13-year career, and Alan Page, who had a 16-year career, were pretty durable. But I did get in the game the week after we lost to Detroit.

We played the San Diego Chargers in Chicago, and Page threw a shoe. I went in, and on my first play for the Bears, it was a running play and I tackled Chuck Muncie.

That's not too bad. But in New England, in an exhibition game, my first sack was against Jim Plunkett. At least I learned some things while I was watching. Alan Page told me something that mattered to me at the end of my career. He saw in practice how I was just full bore, and he said, "Young man, you're going to learn to look at your knees like retreaded tires. The less miles you put on 'em, the longer they last."

As the years rolled on, the immediacy kind of faded and I became the guy making concessions. My knees were having to get drained every week. The old immediate me would've kept playing and practicing and getting the knee drained. I figured out I could practice less, get the knee drained and be healthier for the game. The immediate Mongo didn't give a shit about that—I just wanted to eat.

THE CURB WARRIOR

Up at old Halas Hall, we had a janitor, Richard McMurrin, who used to draw this sarcastic little cartoon for the team to enjoy when we walked into the complex. It was one panel about whatever went on that week, and it was a good thing I could take a joke.

Richard loved to draw me and my dog hanging around. (Cartoon by Richard McMurrin)

Once I got up there and my antics started getting infamous, most every week it'd be one of me.

Since I'd been out of work for six weeks, money was kind of tight. I'd been paying on my Cadillac, on my mother's, and on my house in Austin and trying to help the family, but after New England cut me there were no more checks coming in.

So I was still paying on my mother's Cadillac, but not mine. When I got to Chicago, the car dealer found out that's where I was, so he sent the repo guy to come get it. My Caddy actually got repossessed in the Halas Hall parking lot.

They got it while I was in practice, took all the bags in it and put them in the Halas Hall hallway.

Richard couldn't let that go. This was about the time *Road Warrior* was out—Mel Gibson in one of those post-apocalyptic movies—so McMurrin's comic strip the next week was the Curb Warrior. He draws me in that *Road Warrior* outfit with my foot up on the curb, hitching a ride, with all the bags they left in the hallway behind me.

Richard even got my Great Dane in one of his comics. He drew me and the dog sitting in the Lantern, a bar in Lake Forest. The dog's sitting next to me like my best friend, cigarette hanging out of his mouth and a beer in front of him, and I'm like an old drunk retired guy, extolling the virtues of how I used to play. The thought balloon's over my head and I'm saying, "There I was in St. Louis, kicking ass the way I'd been taught..."

THE COACH BEFORE DA COACH

Neill was a lot like another Bears coach, Dick Jauron. He was laid back, he wasn't a volatile guy, and all the guys liked him because he let them loaf and get away with shit.

That's where the phrase "brother-in-law" first came into my mind. They expected everybody in practice to "brother-in-law," that's half-ass it, so they look good. If you're on the defensive practice team going against the offense during their period, you were expected to brother-in-law.

It didn't make Dan Neal happy when he broke his neck firing off and I didn't give. That's when Jay Hilgenberg started getting his chance and developed into a multiyear All-Pro.

Another similarity between Armstrong and Jauron: The offensive scheme and the way the offense performed that year was terrible. And we all knew he was going to get fired at the end of the year.

STICKING WITH RYAN

At least Buddy Ryan was there—and he had guys like Doug Plank and Gary Fencik.

I remember being in New England, watching tape. The Patriots didn't play the Bears, but we watched our next opponent's offense play against other teams, and sometimes it'd be the Bears.

The way Plank and Fencik were playing safety, just killing guys, the Patriot coaches were probably thinking they were the criminal element in the league. I was thinking, "Hey, I'd fit in there."

I think the old man knew it. If it wasn't for George Halas, I never would have had a career with the Bears. If the McCaskeys had been in charge—that isn't their kind of stuff.

And Buddy, I call him the old fat man, now. In the brotherhood of football, there's people like you on every team, and you find that out. That's how you relate.

That dog thing? Most guys, it would have hurt their feelings. I laughed my ass off. I got it. Like I said, before the year was over, we knew the old man was going to fire Armstrong.

Well, Gary Fencik was a staunch advocate of Ryan at the time. I guess since he went to Yale, he was smart enough to see what some folks didn't.

Buddy is a short man. He wasn't fat, but he had a large frame on a short guy. He's country—still lives in Kentucky raising his horses. And what does everybody perceive about someone who has that country slang? Dumbass.

But he ain't. He's a genius, baby. Very intelligent. That's why his defenses were good, because they were smart.

Anyway, Gary brings this piece of paper around, wanting all the guys on the defense to sign it, to give it to the old man, telling him we wanted him to keep Buddy as the defensive coordinator.

Even though Buddy was just playing me as a backup, I signed the thing. I wanted him to stay around long enough so I could finally impress him enough to play me. Then in my mind, I'd done something.

Chapter 3

THE CAST OF CHARACTERS

CLEAN AND—WELL, CLEAN

Everybody's seen *North Dallas 40*. The core of our team might have been partiers and drinkers and maybe took one too many painkillers, but there was nothing like that going on, as far as drugs go.

North Dallas 40 was a negative view. As far as I'm concerned, we loved what we did and we had fun doing it. Nothing but positive, baby.

But like I said, that was the core. From time to time they'd bring a guy in there who you knew was on drugs. There was this little wide receiver we had one year who would carry his Kleenex box around, know what I'm saying?

But he didn't last very long. The day they cut him, Walter Payton, knowing the press was going to be in there and he was going to be cleaning out his locker, dumped sugar in his locker and made lines like they were cocaine for him. We laughed.

Again, those guys didn't last long.

That's one reason why we were a good team, in my mind—maybe we were characters, but we were characters with character.

DOUG PLANK

I only played with Doug one year, 1981, but he's a good place to start. He was No. 46, and Buddy did call it the 46 defense.

Buddy loved him and loved the way he did his business, so that's why it was the 46 defense. That, and it was built around a safety like Doug making plays.

That's why Todd Bell, more or less Doug's successor as a starter after Len Walterscheid got most of the time in '82, was the MVP of the defense in '84. That's why he held out and the McCaskeys didn't give him the money he deserved. Hell, that's why Dave Duerson stepped right in the next year and became All-Pro. The 46 is tailor-made for the strong safety.

Doug was the nicest guy you want to meet in the world off the field. But I guess he's like me when you put that helmet on. Those jaw pads pinch something up there in that soft spot behind your eyes and you just get vicious.

He used to take out guys in practice like you do in games. I guess that's why our offense stunk back then, because nobody was going to catch a pass over the middle. He used to hit guys so hard he'd knock himself out, and that's what eventually ended his career.

I remember his last Green Bay game. A big old behemoth pulling guard—compared to him—came around. Here goes Doug, forcing the play. He came up, the guy didn't try to cut him, so Doug took him on high. Doug took his ass out—boom, hit him as hard he could. It laid out the guard, but it pinched both nerves on both sides of Doug's neck so badly that all he could do was stand there.

I don't know if you know what it feels like to get a pinched nerve, but your arm goes numb and it feels like hot water running down your arm, and it's dead.

Doug hit that guard so hard it did both sides, and he's standing there, can't move either arm, as the running back runs right beside him. In the film room, we gave him hell for that.

DAN HAMPTON

My first recollection of Dan Hampton? He was a bookworm.

Back in college, he was one year ahead of me in school. He played for the Arkansas Razorbacks, and we were mortal enemies. The first time my team was going to play his, when we were in game planning, there were pictures of the individuals. Dan had bad eyes, and I guess that was before he could get contacts. He had these big, coke-bottle glasses on.

Professor Dan By-God Bookworm.

Later, I'd come to find out I was right. Dan was a voracious reader of novels and had a quiet intelligence. Pretty quick intelligence, too. Dan was my best friend in the game, and the trouble we caused together could fill this whole book—but I'll give you one quick taste.

Once we were going out to one of the bars in Highwood near Halas Hall, sometime in the early '80s. Dan brought his classic Corvette up that year, and we were going out in that.

At the time, the bar we were going to was just selling beer and wine, but they'd let us drink whatever we brought in, so we made up a pitcher of watermelons—a mixed drink most people drink as shots—and took it with us.

On the way, Dan wanted to show me how fast the 'Vette could go, so he was punching it through the suburbs. We went down this one straightaway, and we saw an ambulance up ahead with its lights on. Dan, showing off his fast car, passed it.

Of course, a cop saw it and stopped us. We were arrogant enough to keep the pitcher of watermelons right out in the open.

The cop took the pitcher, set it on top of the car, talking about, "Oh, I've got you guys now. Got the evidence right here."

We had to get out of the car, too. So while Dan was getting out, he grabbed the pitcher, tossed the watermelons out, set it back on the car and said, "What evidence?"

Because we hadn't started drinking yet, he had nothing on us. So we got off.

Even with that kind of ability for mischief, I imagine he got the bookworm thing the whole time in school, because he didn't play football until his senior year in high school. He was in the band. The guy's like a savant with instruments—plays like six different ones to this day.

But when he played against me, the Razorbacks never beat the Longhorns.

By the time I got to Chicago, I hadn't really changed. They had this place you might have heard of called Rush Street. That's when Dan Hampton first started becoming my buddy.

I just got to Chicago and didn't know what was going on, the in places to go to. But I promise you, he did, and he was more than happy to show me. Places like Mothers and the Snuggery and those other bars on Rush Street.

I guess we got along because we were both country boys, small-towners, and had a lot in common. The Bears had a bunch of guys from the Southwest Conference at that time— Mike Singletary, from Baylor, was another one. Being from that Texas conference, it was like a brotherhood, a family. That's the best thing a team of guys can evolve into—thinking of each other as family, because you're going to fight your ass off for family.

Dan Hampton at his last game at Soldier Field.

Danny's just a man's man. His attitude and who he is and what he's about are what impress you. They'd impress any man. It's hard to explain, but he's got the right attitude to survive in this world. If everybody could explain "it," then everybody could get "it." But "it" is indefinable. And he's got "it." Like a movie star.

Thank God he was on the team at the time. He became my big brother, my guide through chaos, really. It especially motivated me in practice to dominate and kick ass. Impressing him was a big factor. I wanted to show him that I was one of the brotherhood, that I fit in with what he considered important about playing football. Every guy who plays that smash-mouth brand of football is impressing other guys who do.

Hampton thought he was in charge of nicknaming guys. His nickname for Brad Shearer was "Snarler," because Brad was this big old guy and when he'd get drunk, you couldn't hear him talk. You'd just hear him going, "Rarrr, rarr."

Dan was the guy who nicknamed me Mongo, because he saw me trying to knock the horse out in practice, figuratively speaking. You know in *Blazing Saddles*, Mongo rides his bull into town, hitches it up by the saloon. A guy rides up on a horse. "You can't park your bull there." I mean, the audacity. So Mongo knocks his horse out.

In practice, there were some things you might let go—if you weren't quite so immediate as me. Say you'd get free of a guy rushing the passer and he'd just grab you and pull you back. With me, after the grab and the pull, wham, a forearm to the head would follow—and the fight was on.

That's how I got Mongo.

Dan gave me "Ming," too. "Ming the Merciless," like in Flash Gordon. That one meant a lot to me, like getting Buddy Ryan to stop calling me by my number. Mongo was something Dan thought was funny. Ming was a sign of respect.

MIKE SINGLETARY

I've heard a lot of people say Mike wasn't much of an athlete, that he was more about film study. Come on. He was a consensus All-American in college, a middle linebacker who could run from sideline to sideline and catch anybody. He had talent. He didn't have the height that Brian Urlacher does—but everybody can see, when Brian has to take on a block, how that height works against you.

I always loved playing against guys taller than me, because I could get under them and they weren't going to move me anywhere.

But, yeah, Mike was a brilliant student of the game, too.

If you know what you're looking for, if you've gone over so much film, you see the tendencies over the years of an offensive coordinator or a coach to do things. When it comes down to nut-cuttin' time, you can decipher a play.

Mike would call out plays in a game when they'd get to the line of scrimmage. He's the only one I've ever known in my football career who was adept at doing that. There were times, when it was blatant, that I could do it. But Mike had a propensity for it.

I've called him the cheap-shot Christian—and I meant it as a compliment, but I think I need to revisit that. I think God Almighty is a football fan. He sits up in the big press box in the sky, drinking a beer, having a hot dog, watching the game. He's not too concerned who's going to win.

Now, you know there's guys who get in the locker room and pray for the win, but Singletary didn't do that. The guys who pray for the win are praying to the devil, you know?

Singletary prayed, too, and then he'd go out there and try to break somebody's neck—which is why I called him the cheap-shot Christian. But when everybody would go in the shower and pray and hold hands before a game, part of Singletary's prayer was, "God help both teams stay healthy."

He was just praying to God that God didn't let him hurt nobody. That's the best part. "I'm going to go out there and be vicious, but don't let me hurt nobody."

Mike and Al Harris were men of their convictions when it came to religion. They weren't selling wolf tickets about it; that's who they were. You can see guys who don't mean it for one fucking minute get in front of the cameras and go, "Oh, I want to thank God and my teammates." That's rhetoric. Mike meant it.

Me and religion? Let's just say I always knew that you can be forgiven. I always talked to my God afterward and said, "I'm sorry."

But I did go to Mike's church one time, just to see what it was about, and he got mad at me because I put it in the papers. Organized religion is about tithing, brother. The first thing out of the box at his church, the first prayer, "Oh, God, please let these people know we need them to put money in the collection plate." I almost got up and left.

Mike didn't like that at all, me talking about his church.

OTIS WILSON
AND WILBER MARSHALL

These two together with Mike were what we called the Bermuda Triangle, those three linebackers.

Otis and Wilber, to me, were the same. They were singular—a vicious brand of howling dog. They'd get on either side of me, and that's how the dog pound got to barking—we did it first in Chicago because of Otis and Wilber.

Everybody sees this on TV—the guys talking smack to each other as the offense is getting the call and coming out of the huddle. That shit wasn't going on, but we'd get the defensive call and Otis and Wilber would be standing there barking at the offense, like pit bulls. Actually, I called Otis the doberman pinscher and Wilbur the pit bull.

If there's one mean dog in the pack, they're all going to be mean. That's what Otis and Wilber afforded us. Sometimes you see teams and one week they're up, the next they come out of the locker room flat. When Otis and Wilber got to playing the game the way they played it, that was impossible.

If the team was flat coming into the first quarter, after a couple of downs of them kicking the shit out of people and barking about it, the team wasn't flat any more.

Don't think Singletary didn't do it either, before the game. Before the game, they'd get together in a three-man hug, and they weren't praying. They were barking.

RICHARD DENT

Nobody wanted him because he was so skinny coming out of college. But Richard set the school record with 39 sacks at Tennessee State—and Too Tall Jones went there before him.

Dan and I recognized it right off in practice. The kid didn't have a clue how to talk football or perceive it, but it was like that photographic memory, that savant thing. You put him out at defensive end, from day one, here comes the play, and he'd make the right decision. Instinctively.

Richard was an amazing athlete. I only see Urlacher jumping over guys in commercials. Richard did it on the field, and we tried to allow for that.

Dan and I and Buddy Ryan, and later Vince Tobin, kind of let Richard play his own game out there. It wasn't predeter-

Defensive line coach Dale Haupt surrounded by Dan Hampton, Richard Dent, me, Jim Osborne, Mike Hartenstine and Tyrone Keys.

mined that he had to rush outside. He had the leeway to go inside or out, and we adjusted.

Mike Singletary would call the defensive plays; Dan and I would call the line stunts. That wasn't typical, but the coaches trusted us enough to see things like a coach up in the press box calling down to the sideline. We already knew it.

I knew Richard was going to rush the passer, so whatever line stunt I wanted to call, I had to make sure we had some cover on that side. I just couldn't run Dan and me to the left side and leave a big gaping hole over there between him and Richard— because that's where the quarterback is going to step up in the pocket and have a clear field of vision to throw the ball.

Seems like it worked out most of the time.

GARY FENCIK

They called us the dichotomy of the league, me and the Ivy-Leaguer, the Bulldog from Yale—a guy who was on the cover of *GQ*, for God's sake.

We'd go do that Crain's Quarterback Lunch, a paid speaking gig on our day off during the week, and that's how they billed us. It was theater with the redneck and the conservative Republican. I always told him, though, when Daley's ready to get out of there, I'll vote for him for mayor of Chicago.

But on the football field, he was more like Doug Plank. He had split personalities, a paranoid schizophrenic—and you'd better believe paranoia plays a part of it when you're talking about a DB. I better get my ass deep or I'm gonna get burned—that's paranoia.

Sometimes, though, that Doug Plank in him got the better of Gary.

When we used to have training camp in Lake Forest, we'd go to this row of bars in Highwood. This particular event happened at the Silver Dollar. Dan and I were not too bad at shooting pool, and we were owning the table. Little Gary Fencik was getting pissed off about it.

Finally he came up to Dan and me, pissed off, drunk—conservatives get drunk, too—and says, "You two assholes, if I was as big as you, I'd whip your ass."

We looked at him and said, "Gary, but you ain't." We grabbed him and dragged him out the back exit door into the alley and just started dragging him around. We showed him he's not as big as us, he shouldn't have said it, and please don't ever say it again.

The asphalt left him cut and bleeding, and you know how smart he is. He never said anything like that again. But I love Gary Fencik. There's few men have come through my life who I know have got their shit together, and he's one of them.

LESLIE FRAZIER

Corn—we called him that because he was from Alcorn State—is the best cornerback who ever played whom nobody knows, because of what happened in the Super Bowl. He made the best interception I've ever seen in my life, up in Green Bay.

The Packers were down there close to the end zone and the receiver did a button-hook in front of him. Corn jumped up over the guy and did a jack-knife. His stomach was over the guy's head, with his feet behind him. He grabbed it in front of him without touching him.

He was on the way to being in the Hall of Fame.

Unfortunately, we got a little stupid in the Super Bowl on the punt return team. By halftime, the game was over, and I don't know what the thought process was there, but we ran a reverse punt in the second half. Like we needed to, right?

He got the reverse and blew his leg out on the Astroturf. There went his career.

MIKE HARTENSTINE

I don't know what they do at Penn State, but most of the guys come out of there with huge calves. It's unbelievable. Matt Suhey, Mikey, all the other guys I've seen outta there. Huge calves. Must do a lot of toe raises or something.

I love Mikey. The best friend you'd want in your life would have Mikey's attitude. And he's of the toughest guys, pain toler-ance-wise, I ever met in my life. Some of the guys I'm talking about with the Bears—Walter, him, Dan, me, the highest pain tolerances you'll ever see.

The bone in your hand that leads up to your thumb? Mikey broke that once. He didn't miss a game, because they went in and pinned it back together. The two pins were sticking out of his hand like antennae, but he played.

Dan, Mikey, and me, all being defensive linemen, hung out a lot. Dan and I are more the gregarious type. Mikey's more laid back—in other words, he doesn't talk much. But that makes sense. With Dan and me around, how could he get a word in edgewise?

We'd call him Mr. Noncommittal. We'd ask him what he wanted to do, he'd say, "whatever."

On the field, though, he was committed. Laid the best blind-side shot I've ever seen on a quarterback—Ron Jaworski of the Eagles. As a result of that hit, he was the first guy I ever heard of getting called to the league office in New York.

The league didn't call the fine down to Chicago. They brought him to the office, put the tape on of him just about killing Jaworski with him sitting there, and said, "This is why we're fining you."

It's kind of out of the ordinary, don't you think? Calling a guy all the way to New York to say, "We're fining you for this. Don't do it again."

What's he gonna say?

"Whatever."

Mr. Noncommittal.

AL HARRIS AND TODD BELL

We played our asses off in '84, finally won that first division championship, got into the playoffs, and lost to San Francisco in the NFC championship game. We knew we were a good team, and the individual guys knew they were good players.

Big Al and Todd Bell's contracts were up. After they've had some success, people are going to start wanting some more money. They were the first ones. That was back before free agency, baby. The teams owned you. The last bastion of slavery in America. If you didn't play for them and they didn't want to trade you or cut you, you sat.

That's what the McCaskeys had them do, I guess to prove a point to everybody else, I don't know. They could've traded them, for God's sake, because they were good players. But they let them sit out the whole year wanting some more money.

We didn't see them the whole year. They were gone. I actually heard Al was living like a hermit in a cave in Arizona—it wasn't true, but I think he kind of liked the story.

When it's all said and done, when it's over, money fades—and fame definitely fades. All you've got is playing the game. Al and Todd, if they had it to do over again, I guarantee they'd have come back and played that year for the money the McCaskeys were offering. Especially since they're not wearing a Super Bowl ring.

To tell you the truth, the defense didn't really miss them. We drafted a kid named Dave Duerson who was sitting behind Bell, and he turned out to be a pretty good player. As for Big Al, well, they'd just drafted the Fridge.

Sometimes that's what happens.

One time Singletary hurt his hamstring and took two games off. Those two games playing behind Dan, Ron Rivera made Defensive Player of the Month in the NFL. Singletary never missed another game.

Ron was good, too. That's what happens when a veteran lets a kid in the door—they find out he can make plays, too.

WILLIAM "THE REFRIGERATOR" PERRY

Fridge was an anomaly back then—over 300 pounds, with a big belly. Today, there's guys playing on every team fatter than him. This guy is more comedian than anybody will ever know. He made me laugh almost every day saying funny shit.

He used to call Ditka the doctor. Not Coach, Mike, Iron Mike—he'd call him the doctor. And I never realized why. Mike Ditka—M.D.—the doctor. Ditka could be on his ass about something, and I guess his defense mechanism was this song. He started singing it all the time.

"Oh, the doctor—cold, bold, and full of what? Soul!"

I don't know why he sang it, but he did.

People have asked me what I thought about the Bears drafting another interior lineman when that was my position. The best way to handle it is you teach the guy what you know and what's going to help you win the game. Any other way, and you're full of shit because you're not trying to win the game.

Besides, the Bears did it all the time. They drafted him, a guy named Fred Washington who ended up killing himself in car wreck, Tim Ryan, Chris Zorich...

You can't have enough good defensive linemen on your team. It just motivates you to play even harder.

Speaking of motivation, the Fridge owes the doctor and the 49ers for making him famous. Commercials, catching a pass and scoring a touchdown in the Super Bowl, none of it would have happened if not for the 49ers rubbing Ditka's face in it when they beat us in the championship game in '84.

They put a guard named Guy McIntyre in the backfield to run out the clock. Like, "We're good enough to play somebody out of position and laugh at you guys." You better believe the next time we played them, Ditka was ready in his mind to show them who'd laugh last. He kept it to himself.

In '85, we went out there and beat them 26-10, one of the best games I played in pro football. Got a game ball, had a guard named Randy Cross jumping offside, I sacked Montana, almost picked off one of his screen passes—just tipped it—had a bunch of tackles. That's when I knew we were going to go to the Super Bowl and win it, when we handed them their ass out in their own stadium.

We were running out the clock, and Mike Ditka, an eye for an eye, puts William in the backfield and lets him carry the ball. It wasn't on the goal line; he didn't score a touchdown. He just handed him the ball and the clock ran out.

But it made such an impact, like a tidal wave over the NFL, it was the only thing anybody wanted to talk about. I guess because a head coach has to be like a carny barker, too, to get a

Relaxing during a practice with the Fridge.

little light shining on his team, Ditka did it again the next week. Plus, he didn't like the Green Bay Packers anyway. So to him, it's, "How can I get everybody talking about my team and stick it in the craw of the Green Bay Packers?"

We got on the goal line, he handed the ball to Fridge, and Fridge scored a touchdown.

In every Shakespearean drama, there's some comic relief. William Perry was ours.

WALTER PAYTON

Emmitt Smith, my ass. That kid ran behind three All-Pros at all times.

Most of Walter's career, until they built a team there in the mid-'80s, he was running behind an offensive line of a bunch of dockworkers. They couldn't blow a fart out a paper bag, and he was still making yards.

Walter was the first guy I ever met who worked harder in the off season than what I'd known. You know how most running backs practice? They get the handoff, it's a brother-in-law thing, they go through the hole, run 20 yards, stop and comes back. Walter would run the whole length of the field, full blast.

In his later years, rookies would come in and try to make a name for themselves by hitting Walter in practice. Who do you think had a problem with that? The bullies' bully—and you don't bully Walter. Plus, I knew he was the show on offense. Without him, we didn't have a chance. Same thing with Earl Campbell down in Texas. That's the franchise. You don't hit the damn franchise in practice.

But the one thing a lot of people don't know about Walter is he was always a prankster.

One of the things he would do—scared the shit out of me every time he did it—he'd get an M-80, low-end dynamite, and he'd tape it to a lit cigarette. He'd go out before practice and plant that M-80 in the grass somewhere around the practice field. Early in practice, it'd go "boom" and it'd scare the shit out of everybody.

Later on, the way he'd show me he respected me, most every day he'd walk up behind me, with me unawares. He'd grab up under my armpits, around my chest, and lock his hands together and squeeze until I'd say uncle. I'm sure he wanted to do it around my neck, but all he could reach was my chest.

I've met Michael Jordan, and of course Walter, and a few other guys people consider superstars. One of the things that defines them is that there's not a stair step to them. There are not different levels of people. They're down to earth. People look up to them like gods, but that's not how they perceive themselves. They don't have the vanity that comes from ego. They know how good they are, but they don't need a pat on the back.

JIM McMAHON

When he showed up in the limo with a beer in his hand, drunk, at his first press conference after getting drafted, I knew our new quarterback was my kind of guy. He wasn't always Dan's kind of guy, which led to the one time I wanted to kick Dan's ass, for real.

It's not his fault, but when people ask me why we didn't win more Super Bowls, I tell them it was Jim McMahon's fault because he was hurt all the time. Jim missed the playoffs in '86. In '87, he got hurt during our loss to Washington in the play-offs. He hadn't played in two months before coming into our first-round win in the fourth quarter in '88, and he wasn't very good and got replaced by Mike Tomczak in the next game, which we lost.

Still, it really wasn't his fault he kept getting hurt. This is what Dan didn't understand. When you're hurt and you're a quarterback and you're getting the shit knocked out of you by guys like Dan and me, if you're hurt already, you're tempting permanent injury by playing against some vicious animals.

I forget what year it was, what playoff game, but Dan stood up in some meeting and said, "Me and Steve are playing on knees that need operations, we're getting them operated on after the season, and we need you to play, man." Calling him out.

I knew right away, man. Anything that can divide a team is better left unsaid. How do you think the offensive guys felt about Dan doing that? "Hey, you defensive cocksucker."

Dan didn't accomplish anything but to divide the team. It pissed me off. I followed Dan up to the locker room and jumped him. It was like a younger brother taking on an older brother—a love thing, you know what I'm saying?

Thing was, everybody thought I was kidding and dogpiled us after that. When William Perry was the last guy on the dogpile, he cracked a vertabrae in Dan's neck—which nobody figured out for years.

Remember Dan's pain tolerance. Years later, somebody X-rayed him and said, "Hey, you had a cracked vertabrae in your neck that healed."

He thought back on it and figured that's when it happened. Dan never knew I was pissed at him. Until now, I guess.

But I knew McMahon had a chance at being nuttier than me when I heard about his retina. He's got a big gash in it—that's why he wears sunglasses all the time—and the story is he stuck a fork in his eye.

Even I won't go there.

You could see in college he was one of those savants—a guy who takes a snap and as he's backpedaling has deciphered where to throw the ball already. It's second nature to them to know where the secondary's rotating to, who's double-teamed, where's man and where's zone. They don't have to go through the progressions like most quarterbacks do.

It's not, "Well, my primary receiver is double-covered," then they start down the line. Who's the secondary? Who's third? It's like photographic memory, and he sees the whole picture at once.

Plus, you've got to like anybody coming in and bucking authority like he did.

THE OFFENSIVE LINE:
Jimbo Covert, Mark Bortz, Jay Hilgenberg, Tom Thayer and Keith Van Horne

I hate to dog the guys who were there before them, but these guys were Walter's first real line. I kind of put them all together, even though Jimbo Covert was the best of them before he hurt his back.

Jimbo's the reason I know anybody can get their ass whipped—I don't care how bad you think you are. He was the only guy in a football practice I ever said "uncle" to.

Something happened in practice he didn't like, and he turned around and thought it was me who did it, so he fired up. Here I come, I'm going to start raining punches on him. Little did I know he was like an All-America wrestler in high school. That's where I learned about the hip toss.

He just grabbed me, turned me, lifted me up and dropped me as he landed on top of me. He wasn't hitting me; he just pinned me there. Well, I couldn't move. Finally I said, "Could you let me up? I give."

You know, this is my book. I didn't have to tell you this. But I just want you to know, there isn't a mortal walking on the face of this earth who can't get his ass handed to him.

Which brings me to Bortzie.

Mark Bortz was drafted at defensive tackle out of Iowa. He wasn't going to make the team until Dan and I mentioned to Mike Ditka that he ought to try this guy on offense. He was pretty stout.

Just going against a guy in drills and he's better than the offensive linemen you're playing against in practice, you should tell the coach, "Why don't you try this guy on the offensive line?" Then he goes on and makes All-Pro.

I kind of did the same thing for Big Cat Williams. You know, "Before you cut this guy, trying to play him at defensive tackle, try him out on offense." And Big Cat went to the Pro Bowl, too.

Practicing is kind of like wrestling sometimes. The body slams are real, but the punches and the kicks are pulled. And you don't go after someone's knees.

So I'm on defense, but it's offensive period. I'm giving Bortzie a picture—a picture of what the other team's defense is going to run against them that week.

It was a rainy day. I found out looking at the film the next day that he didn't do it on purpose; he just slipped in the mud and went down, but when the ball snapped, he fired out and just dove straight at my knees. He hit my legs and just stopped there.

I reached down, and for everybody's enjoyment I was talking real loud, "Get off your knees, son, I'm not God. You don't have to pray to me."

Then I grabbed his facemask and start trying to jerk him up—I'm not trying to help, I'm trying to hurt him. The facemask, in my hand, went, "bink, bink, bink." All four of the bolts broke off the helmet, and I pulled the facemask clean off.

He jumped up, looking like he's Knute Rockne in a leather helmet, and everybody just broke up.

Jay Hilgenberg gave me the best compliment I ever got in my athletic career. He told a reporter once, "Practicing against Steve McMichael and Dan Hampton, the games are easy."

Jay could deep-snap better than anybody. Because of that, popping his arms back that way, his elbows are terrible now. Can't straighten his arms out at all. I feel sorry for him for that, but I know he'd do it all over again.

He had a great career, especially for a guy who was a free agent out of Iowa, making the Pro Bowl seven straight years for the Bears. Lucky for him I couldn't long-snap when they brought me in for that tryout after I got by New England; otherwise he might not have ever gotten the chance.

Keith Van Horne was a good guy, just a little bit different than everybody else. It's that California cool, the surfer mentality—they just think different.

He was a rock 'n' roller, a live-concert guy. I can't stand live concerts. They don't sound as good as they do in the studio.

But it worked out OK for Keith. He ended up marrying Eleanor Mondale—yeah, Walter's daughter—who was working at the rock radio station in town.

You've got to give Tom Thayer credit for timing. The Bears originally drafted him as a center, but they already had Hilgenberg playing there, so Thayer went to the USFL.

I guarantee the USFL was going to pay more money than the McCaskeys were offering him, so he makes his money for two years, jumps to the NFL just before that league folds and just in time to play guard for the Super Bowl champs.

MATT SUHEY

He's another one of those Penn State guys with the big calves. He was one of the ones who had particular glee in what Jimbo Covert did to me that one day in practice. Offense vs. defense, brother.

The first time I ever met Matt Suhey was the Hula Bowl. Like I said, I was the Defensive Player of the Game and he was on the other team—so he already had bad feelings about me.

But for our team, I just think of it this way. In Dallas, Emmitt had Moose Johnston. Well, in Chicago, Walter had Matt. That's a fair parallel, because Moose was pretty damn good.

Matt was another smart guy. Before everybody was into having their own PC, Matt brought his own computer—a car full of computer, in those days—to training camp and set it up in his room so he could keep up with the stock markets. He was into his postcareer activities that early. I believe he and Paterno got into a bottled water company in Pennsylvania, and it made them a fortune.

Yeah, he's a smart dude. But you look back on any good football team, and that's something you hear about them— they're smart.

I promise you, most of the guys on that football team were football literate. Savants for football. A high football IQ. I don't know about their schooling or anything else, but I promise you they had a high IQ for football.

WILLIE GAULT

Every team has to have that deep threat.

Even in the Super Bowl year, Willie Gault didn't catch 40 balls, but I promise you, he spread that defense out thin running down the field. They had to cover him, so there was always something open underneath. Every team needs a speed receiver, and he was that.

Actually, he was more of a Hollywood actor in need of a stunt man than he was a football player. Because you can't have a stunt man, he did it himself. Didn't want to, but to his credit he did. You better believe he didn't enjoy the contact—but what guy who's six feet tall and skinny as a lizard is going to go, "Oh yeah, I want somebody to hit me?"

He wanted football to get him into acting. Football was just necessary to get him there.

DENNIS McKINNON

Silky D was the best receiver on our team, but nobody ever talks about him. He was smooth—one of those guys who never looked like he was running as hard as he could even when he was hauling ass—had good hands, and went over the middle.

He was also maybe the best receiver I've ever seen when it came to blocking, and toughness, and meanness. Man, I used to love watching him crack back on linebackers—he'd knock the shit out of them. It was a beautiful thing. He was a mean little guy.

He also caught seven touchdown passes our Super Bowl year. Walter Payton and Ken Margerum were tied for second on the team with two each, and Willie Gault caught one. Silky was the go-to guy, really.

Plus, he and I had a lot of little jokes in the locker room. I'd turn around and he'd be looking at me in the shower, toweling off like he's enjoying it a little too much, you know? I'd walk by and squeeze his little butt, like, "Oh, that's firm."

You know, men being men. Having fun.

I'll tell you what I think about guys who are homophobic. It's like, "What are you scared of?" You're homophobic, it's like you're in the closet to me.

EMERY MOOREHEAD

He was good. Sure-handed, and he knew who he was supposed to block on every play. Those guys are valuable.

But an All-World talent like Russ Francis, no.

I never understood that, either. Mike Ditka was an All-Pro tight end, but he never had an All-Pro tight end on his team. You'd think he'd have some coaching there, or some play calling, some thought that there's some value in getting the ball to the tight end.

KEVIN BUTLER

Remember, I was a kicker in high school, so I know how flaky they are. I also know they're usually made to feel like they're outside the team, not really football players, and that just never floated with me.

I made a point to be around Butler, to make him feel like one of us. Besides, he was a good player. He was an All-State quarterback who won the state championship in Georgia.

But, yeah, I took him under my wing, baby. Broke one of his once, too.

There was one night in '93 we were playing the Raiders. All Butler's got to do is kick a field goal and we win. Even Howie Long knew it was over. I was on the field goal team, and Howie was standing on the other side of the line of scrimmage saying, "Steve, I've got a new ranch in Montana. See me after the game, I'll give you my number, you can come on up and visit."

I'm all happy, we're going to win the game. But we line up, Butler hooks the damn thing, we lose.

I walked in the locker room, Butler was sitting there crying in his locker, with reporters all around him like the vultures that they are.

So I spread them apart, yank him up and say, "Goddamn it, there ain't nobody else in this locker room that could even attempt trying to make that field goal. Nobody can judge you in here because you missed that motherfucker. Stand up and be a man, stop squalling."

Well, even afterward, when we went out to dinner, he kept it up. I got so fed up with it, I picked him up and threw him across a couple of tables into a booth. He cracked a bone in his forearm.

He had to wear a cast on his forearm for about a month after that, during the season. Nobody noticed, because he was just a kicker.

Chapter 4

THE DAWN OF DITKA

IRON MIKE SUPPLEMENT

After '81, we knew Armstrong was out, and Fencik's petition got the old man to keep Buddy Ryan, but we didn't know who was coming. Then we heard about Mike Ditka.

I knew of him as a player—how he ended up in Dallas, caught a pass in the Super Bowl and then went straight into being their special teams coach. We all thought at the time, when George Halas hired him with so little experience, that there must be something special about this guy.

It's kind of funny, isn't it? The McCaskeys telling Mike Singletary, when he was trying to get a job there on Dick Jauron's staff, that he didn't have any coaching experience? But just being special teams coach, in Papa Bear's mind, that was enough. Guess he was smarter than his grandson.

Anyway, we found out pretty quick about the fiery competitor that Ditka was and knew why the old man brought him in. What a force.

He was a no-nonsense guy right off the bat. His practices were regimented. The whistle blew for each individual skill. And you hustled to the next drill when the whistle blew. He wasn't about that brother-in-law either, baby. He loved guys going live in practice. He knew that was going to make the games easy.

One day early on, he was out there being Iron Mike. Right out of the box, he yelled, "You guys better hustle, or I'll have your ass out of town with a bus ticket and an apple."

After practice, he says, "Everybody huddle up," because he wants to talk to us. So I yell out, "Hurry up, or your ass is out of here with a bus ticket and an apple."

Ditka was not amused. He wheeled on me and said, "That especially means you, McMichael, if you don't keep your mouth shut."

You can joke with Mike Ditka about most things, but when he has a football mind, he has no sense of humor. He meant what he was saying.

The other thing about Ditka was he was a talented person who'd been through it before, so he knew what to look for in players, what they don't have and what they do have. He had an eye for who was a player and who wasn't, for who wanted to play and who didn't—and he started jettisoning the guys who I knew didn't give a shit.

Ditka started noticing me in practice. His comment was, "He does just enough talking to let you know he's around."

Talking is just kicking ass. The talking goes hand in hand with that. If you ain't kicking ass, you ain't talking. Guys who are getting their ass kicked are kind of quiet.

Ditka made sure he didn't have a quiet bunch.

Ditka patrolling the Bears sideline early in his coaching tenure.
(Photo by Daily Southtown; *Tinley Park, Illinois)*

HIGHWOOD HOMESTEAD

In Ditka's first training camp, he got an idea what he was dealing with, and we got an idea what we were dealing with.

We were still in Lake Forest at the time, but it didn't take him long to realize that with all the stories getting back to people from the camp there, he better move all the boys out of town.

I'm sure I played my part in those stories. See, after my first training camp with the Bears, I had a house on my own, in Highwood, closer to the bars—just me and the Great Dane; it was a real bachelor pad, baby.

I've always had a level of intelligence when it comes to staying out of harm's way—I mean getting fingerprinted and mugshot and stuff. I realized I could just go to the bars in Highwood instead of going down to Rush Street and driving home drunk.

I hardly had any furniture in it at all. Had a couple of beds, no bedroom furniture, a couple of couches and a TV. I didn't even have a refrigerator. I'd keep the beer out in the snow. But then, there wasn't much cooking going on in the house. In the kitchen, anyway.

It beat my accommodations that first year with the Bears, when I stayed in a hotel right next to Fort Sheridan—the old North Shore military base. They called the place the Blue Room, because all the walls were blue.

When the year was over, I went back to Austin and the house I had there. I sold it, because I wanted to come back up to Chicago and live during the off season, like I should have done in New England.

I think that was part of the problem with the way the Patriots felt about me. Working out in the off season every day up at the complex is what they want.

STRIKE ONE

There were some good things about '82—that was the year McMahon came in, and even though we were still going through some growing pains, it was the start of me thinking there's something going on here.

Funny thing was, it was the strike we went on that helped me realize we had some guys who cared. We ended up going only 3-6 that year, but we lost our two games before we went on strike. When we went out, in September, we still got together and practiced on our own. If you have guys who don't give a shit, that ain't gonna happen.

Fencik was running the defense—but to tell you the truth, the coaches were giving us the game plans, the plays they wanted us to run, a scripted sheet. They weren't supposed to be doing it, but they were.

As far as the strike itself goes, I was young and didn't know what to expect—but I thought we were doing the right thing, and in my mind, it was, "Oh boy, we're really going to get the owners to bend."

Nothing ended up coming out of it except this thing called "Plan B Free Agency." It was so hokey, something had to happen somewhere else for this to happen there, then something could happen for you. And nothing ever did.

We just lost those game checks for nothing. Seven of them.

We screwed ourselves and we really screwed the fans, because they didn't get their football that year.

But we did win the first game back, at Detroit. Practice makes perfect, you know.

TOASTING A SEASON

Because of the strike, they had a cattle call for the playoffs that year, 16 teams. If we won the last game, in Tampa, we'd get in at 4-5.

Ditka decided to take us to Tampa to acclimate us for a couple of days before the game. Big mistake. This was the last game of the year, a hard year, guys were getting away from their families, the drudgery of what they do every day and a Chicago winter.

Dan Hampton was *Pro Football Weekly's* NFL Defensive MVP in '82 playing defensive end. On the plane, me and Dan were already starting to drink, celebrating his honor.

Let me tell you, a couple days of drinking down in Tampa doesn't lend itself to being in the best shape you can be in to play in the game on Sunday.

You've been playing in cold weather; then you go down to 80 degrees—oh, that's sapping. Every year we'd do that, I'd lose like 15 pounds—and I was in pretty good shape to begin with. I'd always have to have an IV, and I got smarter as the years went on.

Early on, I'd be on the plane and start cramping, and they'd have to rig up an IV solution in the luggage rack above my head and plug me in on the plane. Later on, I'd just go ahead and get the IV, knowing the cramping was coming.

Anyway, we were down there partying, and I really don't think it affected our play, because we played well against Tampa quarterback Doug Williams—until the very end.

FUMBLE! OXYGEN!

They were just letting me get on the field in '82. I wasn't starting yet, but I had four sacks, and one of them was against
Williams in that game. And near the end of the game, I had the
longest fumble return of my career—a 64-yarder.

We got back and sacked Williams, but they'd been on a long
drive and we were starting to get gassed. I was back there to pick
up the fumble.

Now, all the receivers were downfield because it was a pass
play, so there was nobody back there but me. Plus, Jim Osborne,
one of the guys who sacked Doug, was lying on top of him, and
besides, Doug had gotten hurt earlier in the game and was limp-
ing.

I picked up the ball. Sixty-four yards later, Williams caught
me on the five-yard line. He shook off Ozzy, limped down the
field and caught me. If I had scored, we probably would have
won the game and made the playoffs. As it was, the offense lost
yards, kicked the field goal, we went into overtime and lost.

Jay Hilgenberg told me he was on the sideline down on the
end of the field where I was eventually caught. He saw me pick
the ball up with no one around me and immediately thought he
was going to have to snap for the extra point—and he didn't
have his helmet. He had to go get it on the bench on the other
side of the 50-yard line. He ran, grabbed his helmet and ran
back to where he was, and he swore that when he got back there
I still hadn't passed where he'd been before.

Ever since then, I don't know if it was in the back of my
mind or not, but I always figured it was better to fall on the ball
than pick it up and run with it.

A POSTSCRIPT AND A PREVIEW

Y'all remember that story about dragging Gary Fencik through the alley? If not, flip back a few pages. Anyway, Dan and I didn't end our reign of terror when we stopped picking on poor Gary—who asked for it, by the way.

It's training camp, '83, and we were out behind the Silver Dollar in Highwood. Dan was wild. Roughing up Fencik got his blood up—not that it was really about Fencik. It was about how we were going to kick ass playing football that year. Dan turned around and forearm-shivered the driver's side window in my Bronco and just smashed it out.

I knew I better calm him down, so I went around, grabbed him in a choke hold, took him down and held him till he settled down. A minute later, we got in the truck, and he was driving.

Hey, I wasn't going to sit in the glass.

Anyway, we were just late enough to miss curfew. During camp they put us up in the Lake Forest College dorms.

Dick Stanfield was the offensive line coach. I love this guy; when he played with the 49ers he was the only offensive lineman in NFL history to be voted the MVP of the league. But he was a salty old man, and we were always gigging each other in practice.

I'd say, "Old man, you're lucky you didn't play against me. Back then you could head-slap, and I'd have head-slapped you so much your ears would still be ringing."

He'd say, "Well, McMichael, I'd have made sure you got a few more knee operations, 'cuz I woulda cut the shit out of you."

But anyway, it was about 11:30, curfew was 11, and here we came pulling into Lake Forest College. Dick was already walking away from the dorms; he was in between buildings on a sidewalk.

Dan saw him, said, "That motherfucker's going to turn us in. I'll just kill him."

He jumped the curb with the Bronco, started up the sidewalk, hauling ass at Dick. You could tell Dick was an athlete, because he broke down into a hitting position and started shuffling his feet.

Dan didn't slow down. The old man actually had to get out of the way. We passed him, Dan slammed on the brakes, put it park. We left the truck there in the middle of the compound and went up to sleep.

NIGHT RIDERS

When '83 rolled around, I dumped the house in Highwood and moved about a block down and across the street from Halas Hall.

I'd met this kid, Dave Siden, at a Halloween party Dan Hampton had in '81, and we became friends (good friends—Dave ended up being co-best man at my second wedding, to my wife, Misty).

Dave was living in this yellow house right down the street from the fields we had during training camp in Lake Forest. It was like a duplex; the front was an apartment by itself.

Now Dave was a social butterfly, and he had some great parties. At first, he had somebody else living in the front of that house. But the next year, the guy moved out. I was over there so much I was almost living there anyway—waking up on the couch and stuff. I moved in.

So I'm walking to Halas Hall now. Whether I actually slept the night before or not.

One time, Dan, Mike Hartenstine, Henry Waechter and I ended up basically staying out all night. (Henry, by the way, was the second-string guy I let come in during the Super Bowl, and in that series he got a sack and a safety. I tell you, if I'd have stayed in and got that sack and safety, there's a chance I could've been co-MVP with Richard Dent, but I let Henry go in. That's the kind of teammate I am.)

Anyway, Ditka found out about us staying out, because we weren't even close to making curfew. We also weren't even close to sober that morning for practice, come to think of it.

Ditka called us all up on the carpet, up in front of the team, and started, "All right, you night riders..."

He made us do up-downs until we threw up.

Then we went into practice, and Dan was still in pretty bad shape. We went into this nine-on-seven drill, live. The offense came to the line and we all got down; the play started, bodies started moving around, hitting, and Dan was still in his stance. Everybody was boom, boom, boom around him, and Dan was still in his stance.

They got him out of there after that.

DRAFT SPECIAL

The payoff came later, but the draft Jim Finks, Halas and Ditka put together in '83 put us over the top.

Jimbo Covert and Willie Gault in the first round; Mike Richardson, who ended up being our starting left cornerback for six years, in the second; Dave Duerson in the third; Tom Thayer in the fourth; and Richard Dent and Mark Bortz in the eighth.

Unbelievable. Dent and Bortz, All-Pro, from the eighth round?

You've got to ask yourself, "Why did those people make those picks? What was it all about?"

I think they drafted heart.

Those guys were athletes, but obviously they weren't first-round draft-pick athletes. Those guys wanted to play ball.

That's one thing Ditka could do—he could see a guy who had heart.

BUDDY SYSTEM

Playing kids was never Buddy Ryan's greatest strength. If it wasn't for Mike Ditka, Buddy might never have played me—and Ditka finally made Buddy start me, in the eighth game of '83.

Buddy was just an old coach who was loyal to his own—to a fault, really. Dave Duerson was a great example of that.

Dave came in that great '83 draft, and that year they cut Lenny Walterscheid, a veteran safety whom Buddy liked—a backup to Fencik. He knew if Walterscheid had to play, he wasn't going to make any mistakes, because Lenny was smart—and Buddy valued smart so much he couldn't bring himself to trust young guys not to make mental mistakes, a pretty high priority for the success or failure of each defensive play. But they had to cut Lenny to keep Dave.

When that happened, Buddy came in the meeting and just dressed down Dave in front of everybody.

He said, "Look, I had to let a great player go for you, and I don't think you're worth it. I think you're a piece of shit. So you better get after it."

It was Buddy's defense run Buddy's way, but Ditka's influence was forcing Buddy to realize the loyalty to the veterans was going to hold us back because there were some kids who wanted to play and who were busting their asses. He'd tell Buddy, "Because you're coaching them, you're going to make them great."

BREAKING BAD

Early on in '83, Ditka made some bad decisions. The first one was getting his hair done up in that tight perm he had. Boy, he had some curls. I guess that was to show everybody he was tightly wound.

I really wouldn't put it past him. You'd go up in Ditka's office and you'd see psychology books, not football books. I'm sure that perm was just like "an apple and a bus ticket."

Then there was the fourth game of the season, at Baltimore, which was our second straight overtime loss and dropped us to 1-3. If we'd won, I'm sure he would have been happy to be 2-2.

As it was, he broke his hand on a footlocker.

Where Baltimore played, the Coliseum, it was one of those small locker rooms, no place to store the chests all our stuff goes in, so they were just taking up space in the aisles. Ditka was standing by one when he launched into his postgame tirade. When he finished, he turned around and just punched the shit out of one of those footlockers, and then grabbed his hand.

He'd been on a cussing tirade this whole time—and with Ditka, it was clearly a choice. He wasn't one of those guys who, just talking, would go, "This fucking thing," or, "Goddammit." He doesn't use cuss words, generally. He's not casual with it.

When they'd start coming out, though, it was, "Boom-boom-boom, baboom-boom-boom."

So he wheeled and punched the chest. All of a sudden, tirade's over.

Holding his hand, he just turned to our head trainer, Fred Caito, and says, "OK, Freddy. It's time for the Lord's Prayer."

Then he went into the trainer's room.

METHOD TO HIS MADNESS

We should have known that Ditka's arteries were getting clogged back then because of the beet-red face he'd get. Before he'd start a tirade, you'd know he was fixing to chew on somebody's ass when that face was shining like a beacon.

He'd get on individuals; he'd get on the team. Most of the time it was about what the team was doing. But if you saw him ragging on an individual, it was based on his theory about personality types.

Ditka believed in motivating based on what your personality was. Those guys who needed a pat on the ass, you wouldn't see him cussing them. But the guys he knew it would put them in a rage and they'd say, "Well, I'll show you," he got what he wanted. They'd go out, bust ass, come back and say, "See? I told you."

A START, AND THE BEGINNING

I started the last nine games in '83 and finished the year with eight and a half sacks. We went 6-3 over those games, and 5-1 in last six.

Coincidence? I think not.

No, seriously, a lot of things started to come together.

Willie Gault really started to open things up on offense, and they were starting to catch up to the defense. When he was streaking down the field, it opened up underneath; then you've got Walter—uh-oh, gotta watch him.

All of a sudden Jim McMahon was completing 60 percent of his passes, Willie was catching eight touchdowns on the year and Walter was still Walter, running for 1,400 yards.

Everybody loves talking about our defense—but remember, in '85, our offense was the highest-scoring offense in the league. I know that we on defense were setting them up and scoring some touchdowns ourselves, but Chicago hadn't known that kind of offense before. Not since that 73-0 game against the Redskins for the league championship in 1940.

A great old guy from the '63 championship, Ed O'Bradovich, still talks shit about how bad the offense was on his team. He was a defensive end, and he claims that whenever he'd run off the field when the offense was coming on, he'd say, "Just hold 'em, boys."

WHERE'S MY KICKING SHOE?

One thing from '83 that won't be going on my resumé was the resumption of my kicking career.

In college, I kicked some extra points and field goals when our kicker, Russell Erxleben, was hurt, so when the Bears' Bob Thomas tweaked his back, the put me into duty on kickoffs.

I did it for two regular-season games, so somebody got the bright idea of seeing if I could get a little something for the effort. Everybody was saying, "If I were you, I'd go up there and ask the McCaskeys for a little bump for doing this."

I went up there and they said it was covered in my contract under "football."

Maybe so, but they got more than they paid for. For my two names of glory, I averaged deeper kicks than Eddie Murray, the All-Pro kicker that year. Kicked his little ass.

THE PASSING OF AN ICON

In the middle of the '83 season, George Halas died. It wasn't expected, but he was 88 years old, so it wasn't a surprise either—but in Chicago, you'd better believe it was a very big deal.

I can't remember how many people showed up at his funeral, but it was almost everybody. The whole team went to the funeral. Everybody in the football world went to the funeral.

The multitudes of people, the respect for George Halas are things I'll never forget.

I hope nobody forgets he was the man who invented pro football, the man who had the first team in the league—no matter what they say up in Green Bay.

DIE, PACKERS, DIE

One truly great thing happened in '83. I got my first win over Green Bay.

I'd been around for the second of two losses to the Packers in '81—at Lambeau Field—and we didn't play at all in '82 because of the strike. We lost again at Lambeau in '83, and by the time we got ready to play the Packers in the last game of the year, I was getting a pretty good idea how much it meant.

I mean, I knew the animosity the fans had for them, but I didn't know the depth of hatred of somebody who'd played against them and known the rivalry. Ditka had it. He hated them.

I hated them, too, but I loved the game. It's like in wrestling—there's no show, the fans don't care, unless there's a feud. Without that, it's just another match.

Plus, being a student of the game, playing in Lambeau Field and Soldier Field, that was the shit to me. It's like you're unbound. Like living in every age. Ditka said it once about me, and I think he applied it to anybody he considered a true Monster of the Midway: He could've played in any age.

Playing in a Bears-Packers game made you feel that way.

ALL KNEES ARE NOT CREATED EQUAL

The last game of the year, against Green Bay, my knee was hurting. I got a sack at the end of the game, and instead of landing on the quarterback, if you're watching the film you just see me kind of spin him down by his shirt and limp off the field.

I needed an operation at the end of the season, and it was probably the first example of Mike Ditka working on me.

There was this great surgeon in East Lansing, Michigan, named Lanny Johnson—he was like the keynote speaker at orthopedic surgeon conventions, that kind of thing.

That's where they sent Hampton, who, as usual, needed a knee done at the end of the season. I mean, the guy ended up with something like 12 surgeries. I look like a piker with my eight.

The guy they assigned to operate on me was the team surgeon up in Lake Forest we called Butch, short for Butcher. I go to Ditka, "Coach, can I go to the good one?"

He says, "Steve, you're just not one of our stars."

In the off season, working out, I felt something in this knee. Butch went in there and cut some out, but he didn't look around and find everything.

When I got to camp, two-a-days, pounding it, the knee started to swell up again. With tears in my eyes, I said, "Coach, the season's fixing to start and my knee's already bad. I've got to get it worked on."

Ditka understood the intensity of the Bears-Packers rivalry. (Photo by Daily Southtown*; Tinley Park, Illinois)*

They sent me back to Butch again—and three weeks later I started in the first game of the season.

But don't think I'm complaining. There's a line from D.H. Lawrence that goes, "I never saw a wild thing sorry for itself."

That hits me pretty hard. I'm talking about all these injuries, but I ain't sorry for myself. I had to play. Come hell or high water.

Especially in 1984.

FIRST STOP, NOWHERE

I know why Ditka did it. He was thinking, "We're gonna get these guys away from their norm so they can really concentrate on football." So he brought us out to Platteville, Wisconsin, population 9,708, in territory that's not only more Packer than Bear country, it's more Iowa Hawkeye, too.

Not that it mattered. We got real popular in town, real fast. All Ditka really did was let married guys loose from their families. In Lake Forest, you might see the night riders down on the bar row in Highwood, but in Platteville you started to see married guys out, too. Before, everybody was going home to their family. You'd go to Platteville like you were on vacation from all that.

It was all good, healthy fun. Boys will be boys, you know?

Every year we'd have a post-training camp party at one of the bars in town. There'd usually be some hijinks going on in there, baby. One year, this place had a tile floor, McMahon just soaked the whole floor with a couple of pitchers of beer and says, "All right, we're having McMahon Olympics."

Everybody took their pants off, naked from the waist down, and we had a butt-sliding competition across the floor. I believe

McMahon won—but then, the guy who picks the competition has usually done it before. He was adept at it.

Some people claimed Platteville was boring, but not to me.

Practice was a joy, baby. I love every aspect about that game. Preparing for it and playing it are the same. When they say I even loved wind sprints, it's kind of the truth, because when you were tired after practice and Ditka still ran you, it was like measuring up to yourself.

I'm tired. I make myself take another step. I'm proud of myself. Pushing through the limits, that's what makes the games easy.

BEWARE THE SAVAGE ROAR

Even before the 8-8 year, we thought of ourselves as a lot better team than that already. Heading in, we knew we almost went to the playoffs in the strike year, so we expected to do better than that and be in the playoffs. For whatever reason, we didn't... but we knew we were a good team. Not a great team, but we knew we were competitive. And we came ready to compete in '84.

That was the year we set the sack record—72 sacks—that no one has even gotten close to and no one will. With the West Coast offense, there are no more seven-step drops. Until they get back to the seven-step drop and the pocket passer, nobody will have a chance to get to a quarterback 72 times in one season.

Buddy Ryan realized we had the guys on the defense to attack the offense whenever he chose. Whatever stage of the game, bring 'em, attack the quarterback.

Most coordinators run a blitz so somebody will be set free; there won't be anyone to block him. Buddy would run a blitz for the opportunity to get one of us one on one with a blocker. He used to tell Dan and me in the meeting rooms, "Why the fuck didn't you get to the quarterback? We ran a blitz and got you single-teamed."

People assume it was Buddy's system that did it, but we were system and personnel. That's why nobody's been able to duplicate what we did. We had the personnel to run it up front, which means at least three defensive linemen who can get to the quarterback.

Without that, you'd better sit back in zone coverage and wait for the offense to make a mistake. All the great attacking defenses had at least two ass kickers on the line. The Fearsome Foursome had Deacon Jones, Rosey Grier and Merlin Olsen. The Steel Curtain had L.C. Greenwood, Dwight White, Mean Joe Greene and Ernie Holmes. Even the Purple People Eaters had Alan Page at tackle and Carl Eller and the guy who ran the wrong way, Jim Marshall.

Three guys up there kicking ass, that's what we had, with Richard getting 17 1/2 sacks, Dan 11 1/2 and me 10. We called it a jailbreak. Three or four guys just running at the quarterback—it looked like cons jumping the fence and hauling ass.

It wasn't arrogance. We weren't full of ourselves, but we were confident. The other team played our game.

And here's the proof that we had the personnel: We set the sack record with Buddy Ryan in '84, he left after '85, and Vince Tobin come in with his scheme and we set the scoring record.

SALLY, DICK, JANE AND BUDDY

Buddy Ryan's plans were easy to read for everybody. While most defensive coordinators have all these hand signals, Buddy Ryan most of the time would just clap his hands. That meant AFC— Automatic Front and Coverage. We had to be more intelligent and more responsible to play in Buddy's defense.

During the week we studied up on the opposing formations and what plays they ran out of those formations. It was understood that we already knew the best defense to get in based on their formation instead of the coach calling something on the sideline and hoping they'd come out in that formation.

That was the genius of Buddy's defense. The guys on the defense got into the best defense possible to go against the formation that came out of the huddle. Most defensive coordinators are guessing when they call a defense on the sideline. Buddy didn't have to guess, because, in all instances, when they came out of the huddle and got into a formation, we would shift.

For example, if the other team got in a "blue" formation— the fullback on the tight end side—in our automatic front and coverage, the defensive line knew to shift over from a 4-3 into an "over." That's the defensive end on the tight end, a tackle in the guard-tackle gap, a tackle over the center. Buddy didn't have to call it. But everybody's got to know their shit, because if one guy reads it wrong, you're fucked.

Of course, it helped Buddy that we were all pretty versatile players, so he didn't have to use the personnel groupings most defenses do today.

On the line, I called stuff and so did Dan. Mike Singletary was in charge of making sure the linebackers were in their place. Fencik handled the secondary.

AIR DALE

Dale Haupt was our defensive line coach. Usually he wasn't a wild man, but there was this one time in '84 he figured he needed to fire Dan and me up. He still has a scar on his bald head because of it.

We were in warm ups before a game, basic stuff. You come out, split into your groups, and the first thing Dale would do was hike the ball and we'd take off, getting our legs warmed up.

This day, Dale didn't think we were spirited enough, I guess. He looked at us, he looked down at the other team across the way, and says, "Look down there. See those guys? They're going to whip your asses."

Dale learned the unmitigated rage Dan and I carried into each game. We look at each other like, "Oh yeah? Let's teach this old man a lesson."

Next time he got down like the center between us at defensive tackle and snapped the ball, with my right forearm and Dan's left, we hit him at the same time and flipped his old ass over so hard that the back of his head was the first thing to hit. The Astroturf turf-burned his head.

He got up, and Hampton and I said, "Now say something about the other team again."

GETTING AHEAD OF OURSELVES

In '84, we went 10-6, we won that first division championship. That was our expectation. I think that's why we lost to the 49ers in the NFC championship game. That wasn't our goal. We'd done what we set out to do.

Beating the Washington Redskins the game before was kind of like the highlight, the culmination of everything we worked to do. They were the previous Super Bowl champions, and we went to their house and whipped their asses.

Joe Theisman was the quarterback, John Riggins was at running back, the Hogs were on the offensive line—and we stuffed them. In the fourth quarter, especially, they had a chance to beat us, but we stuffed them and we won, 23-19.

In the locker room after the game, it was an emotional high. We were jumping around like we just won the Super Bowl, because we'd just beaten the defending Super Bowl champs in their own stadium.

Plus, we'd just pulled off the Bears' first playoff win since that '63 championship. Nobody was saying, "Slow down." Everybody was caught up in it. And as high as we were, we should have known there'd be a low to match it.

It happens to this day. You've got to really be conscious of that and defend against it, or you're going to be an up-and-down team and you're screwed.

HEY, GATORADE, WHERE'S MY CUT?

When Ditka first came to town, he was going around drinking with Hampton and me. He was like a buddy. He hadn't gotten into the state of mind where he had to separate himself from the players yet. We were drinking buddies, talking about the future. After a while, he separated himself.

But in '84, we were still in that mindset, and that's when Dan and I came up with the Gatorade bath—and it's time we got the credit. You always hear the Giants invented it. Credit the obvious East Coast media bias in this country. But it was us; they just followed suit.

At the away game in Minnesota, where we clinched the division, our plan was basically, "All right, Dan, you go get the Gatorade jug and I'll stand in front of him and keep his attention." So I stood in front of him as the game was still going on, and he was protesting, "Get away from me." He couldn't figure out why I was talking to him when he was trying to run a game.

I actually had to grab his shoulders and hold him, and Dan came up from behind and just doused him. That's when the

Gatorade baths started. Hampton and I invented it, but we only did it once. Then Harry Carson and the Giants started doing it every game—and oh boy, what a splash it made. If you ask me, the Giants were fabricating character and we had it.

THE POX RETURNS

Coming into the '84 NFC championship, we really thought we were going to dominate physically in that game.

But like I said before, Joe Montana is a pox on my football career. He started in college, when his Notre Dame team beat our asses when I was a sophomore, and this was the next time he got me.

It could've been worse, though. I could've been beaten by someone I don't consider to be the best quarterback of all time. Joe Montana does something I've never seen anybody else do, and I've watched enough film to know. In a three-step drop, not a seven-step, he reads four receivers.

Anybody else you can mention, the most they'll do is three before the rush gets to them or they run. He reads four, and the fourth check down would usually be Roger Craig. He'd dump it to him—not a bad place to check down, considering Roger Craig had better than 1,000 yards catching the ball. That made him hard to get to and harder to rattle.

In fact, I really only tried to rattle him once, and it was in that game.

We were in the 46, and the guard and the tackle blocked on me. I knew it was coming, and I knew they were trying to show us they could be physical, too, so I used it to my advantage.

I leaned my shoulder in there like I was going to try to split them, but when the tackle came down hard I spun around, with my arms spinning too, and caught him head-high with my forearm. Now he was out of my way and blocking the guard for me. I came around free, there was Joe, I sacked him.

It was the first series of the second half, still a close game, so I tried to intimidate Joe into being a pussy the rest of the game. I got up, looked at him and said, "Suck on that, motherfucker." He didn't get intimidated. He got pissed off. He didn't say anything; he diced up our defense.

Six different guys on the 49ers that day caught a pass of at least 10 yards.

I never talked shit to Joe after that.

REMEMBER HOW BAD THIS HURTS

After we lost in the NFC championship, we came in on the plane and the core of the team went to Z Sports Tap. Fencik, Hampton, some offensive guys—all the boys. About 10 or 12 of us altogether.

There were some steps inside the place, and we were all sitting on them like it was a team photograph—a pretty sad one at that. It could have been a trip downtown to drown our sorrows. It could have been a party—most people, if they didn't have the goal to get where they did, so what if they get beat? It's like, "Party time. So what? We got beat. We went farther than we were supposed to."

Nobody expected us to be playing the San Francisco 49ers in the NFC championship game, including us. And it probably didn't bother anyone but us that we lost.

But boy, it hurt. Crushing. That's one of the first instances I knew we weren't going to be a one-year deal. It mattered to these guys. I remember Gary Fencik saying, "Remember how this feels. How bad this hurts."

Chapter 5

THE SUPER SEASON

THE PRESEASON

I don't know what this says about how hard Ditka's training camps were, or how bad our backups were, but our preseason was hardly a precursor to greatness, that's for sure. We went 1-3, and we lost the first three.

It did seem like teams were starting to treat us differently—like we were everyone's homecoming game. We'd see teams running their goal-line offense or their No. 1 field goal team to get the points.

But even if we weren't playing like it, we were starting to get treated like stars. Because we'd won in '84, the training camps were starting to get ridiculous with how many people would show up every day—I'm talking thousands of people.

We were proud of the crowds, but it's hard, man. After practice, when there's little kids standing around and you know your day is still full of meetings, and you've got to eat lunch or get a nap—it's hard to not walk by them.

I'd stand there for a while and sign a bunch of autographs, but when you leave you always leave somebody behind. That's just bad. I never liked doing it. Whenever I do an appearance now, I'll stay until the last person standing there gets his autograph.

I can't stand it when an athlete or a celebrity has a two-hour appearance, and when that two hours is up they get up and leave. If there's people still standing in line, that guy's an a--hole.

Then again, the celebrity isn't always the only one.

We were guys who liked going out and having a good time, brother, and it started getting where you couldn't go anywhere. That's when I realized not everyone's your fan, even though they come up with a smile on their face. Being young and immediate, sometimes it was hard not to hit some condescending shithead right in the face.

For instance, there was one time when I was at the pool hall, playing doubles with my lady, a friend, and his lady. By now, out in public, I'm like the Terminator, always looking around—and I could always see the guy who's going to come up and say something. There's a little clique, they're all looking at you, and sooner or later one of them's coming up with a smile on his face. You know, the red-horned devil can't steal a soul if he comes up looking like that, you understand?

They won't come up and say, "Steve McMichael, nice to meet you." They'll come up and say, "Steve McMichael, what's your secret? I always see you with women." That's what this one guy did.

Most guys might take that as a compliment. But this guy meant it like, "I don't give a shit who you are, but if I had your secret, I could have beautiful women, too."

I told the guy, "Grow six inches taller so you don't look like a midget. Get your hair cut so you don't look like a Chernobyl victim. Change the way you dress, because girls don't like that lumberjack look, and change your rap, because you didn't even fool my ass."

The guy walked off with his tail between his legs.

The fans and the people who care about you aren't the only ones coming out of the woodwork. The jealous ones do, too. Fans aren't condescending. They might want to come and meet you, but they say hello then leave you alone. The jackasses come to get a bite, like a shark feeding.

Now, I'm not the kind of guy who thinks I'm better than anybody else. But then, the opposite of that is ain't nobody better than me, either.

I had to learn to stop being immediate, because there's haters out there.

GAME 1: BEARS 38, TAMPA BAY 28
September 8, Soldier Field

I remember getting booed at halftime at Soldier Field, walking into the locker room down 28-17. Some great start, huh?

I really believe we came into the year with dead legs. I loved Ditka's training camps, but they were brutal. That might have had something to do with giving up four first-half touchdowns.

The Bucs did, too. They had a good team back then, really. James Wilder was at running back, and Steve DeBerg, their quarterback, could decipher a defense.

But we came out after the half, Richard Dent tipped a pass thrown out to the flat and gave Les Frazier just enough time to break on it, catch it and score—a 29-yard interception return. With that we went ahead and ran them out of the stadium after that—we shut them out in the second half.

On the other hand, Wilder had a huge day—166 yards on 27 carries. He just ran all over the field on us.

Ditka and Buddy Ryan, people say they were different coaches, but they adhered to the same standard. You're never as bad as you look when you lose and you're never as good as you look when you win.

When you win, they're going to come in the meeting bitching about plays you didn't make—and we didn't make plenty that game.

GAME 2: BEARS 20, NEW ENGLAND 7
September 15, Soldier Field

My first crack at my old team.

Back then, I downplayed it, but inside there was a fire. These guys had told me I wouldn't be any more than a backup in the NFL—that's if I were to catch on with another team. You better believe I wanted to show them they were wrong.

We all had something to prove, really. The week of meeting speeches might have had an effect on us. We might have come out a little pissed off after getting our asses chewed on for a week.

They had 27 yards rushing, we had six sacks—but I'll tell you, the biggest stat that stands out to me was they only spent 19 seconds over the 50-yard line all day.

That's domination.

OK, so I didn't get a sack. Mike Singletary had three, and Otis Wilson, Wilber Marshall and Richard Dent had one each. But listen, baby, the position I played in the 46 defense, it was pretty tough. I was right in that gap between the guard and the tackle, and those two guys make sure you don't go nowhere first.

Anyway, we beat a good team—shit, they went to the Super Bowl.

GAME 3: BEARS 33, MINNESOTA 24
September 19, Metrodome

Ah, the Vikings game on Thursday night, baby. Everybody remembers this one because this is the one McMahon came off the bench and led us to victory on national TV.

They're beating us 17-9, McMahon is hurt, he's not gonna play. Seems to me it was a kidney or something—I don't know, with him, take your pick.

I don't know if I should tell this on him, and I don't want anything negative about the boys in this book, but he wasn't supposed to play, remember. So, yeah, he'd been out all night. Smelled like alcohol, you know? Might have been why he got in the game. Allegedly, I mean—because I was in my room fast asleep, getting ready for the game the next day.

Anyway, we were losing and he was over there in Ditka's ear so much that Ditka was tired of having him on the sideline, so he put him in the game so he wouldn't have to listen to him no more.

The first three passes he threw were touchdowns—70 yards to Gault, 25 yards to McKinnon and 43 yards to McKinnon. We went on to win the game. I think that was the beginning of the Jim McMahon folklore.

Fuller was 13 of 18 for 124 yards in that game, and he was a good quarterback, but every great team's quarterback is *somebody*, you know what I'm saying? Except for maybe a Bill Parcells team that wins the Super Bowl with a Jeff Hostetler or something.

A commanding presence. When I talk about the difference between Jim McMahon and Steve Fuller, I'm not talking about athletic ability, I'm talking about presence—the kind of person who everybody knows is around.

It's like when you're at the high school dance and the most popular girl walks in the gym, all eyes turn to her.

I always seemed to play better against the Vikings, Packers, and Cowboys.

Besides McMahon, Kevin Butler had four field goals that night. It was like all phases were starting to come together.

Kevin never made All-Pro as a kicker because he kicked so often in Soldier Field. But the All-Pros realized how difficult it was to kick there, because when they'd come in, Kevin would out-kick them.

And I got two sacks. Finally!

You know, there were some teams like the Vikings, the Cowboys and especially the Green Bay Packers, where usually I'd have some stats. I don't know what that's about, but most players have certain teams they play better against.

Besides, statistics are for losers, baby, and this game was a great example. Tommy Kramer threw 55 passes that day. Of course there was an opportunity to get a sack or two.

On the other hand, take a look at the defensive film of the Super Bowl sometime. The first half, there's hardly any film on the reel.

I mean, I had 44 tackles in '85. In '89, when we went 6-10, teams were on the field all day against our defense. I had 108 tackles. In '85, our defense was so good and our offense was good, there were about 50 plays for the other team's offense on the field while ours was out there 75 or 80. You don't have the opportunity for stats.

GAME 4: BEARS 45, WASHINGTON 10
September 29, Soldier Field

The year before, they were the defending Super Bowl champions when we knocked them out of the playoffs in their place; now they came to ours and we gave them their worst beating in 24 years.

Because of that game in the playoffs the year before, we had them beat down. Of course, I think because of those two games, they beat us in the playoffs the next couple of years because they had their dander up.

There's a shot of me from that game, just freight-training Joe Theisman, that ended up on a bubble gum card. I'm on my knees, pushing him down, and he's on his back with his legs up in the air.

Sorry, Joe.

You know, I'd like to tell every quarterback I ever played against it was just that thay had the other uniform on. That's the way I built up my rage, by hating them. But that's all over now. They don't have to hate me still.

Anyway, they got up 10-0 right off the bat, then Willie Gault ran a kickoff back 99 yards for a touchdown. That's kind of the way it went that year—teams would play with us, then we'd start making some big plays and they couldn't keep up. We set the team record with 31 points in the second quarter, seven of them on a pass from Walter Payton to Jim McMahon, which was kind of fun.

As a team, we were kind of like a school of sharks, always fixing to frenzy. One of 'em gets a bite, then all of a sudden everyone's swimming real fast and bitin' stuff.

GAME 5: BEARS 27, TAMPA BAY 19
October 6, Tampa Stadium

Another game, another come-from-behind win. That's why we weren't really getting a lot of attention yet, because we were always coming back.

The Bucs were up in this one 12-3 at halftime. I guess we still had dead legs from training camp; I don't know. We were actually losing 12-0 at one time, but all the details of the game have faded for me except one.

Walter was already 31 years old this season, in his 11th year in the league—an awful long time for a running back. But he made a move in the fourth quarter to score a touchdown that you don't see anybody except maybe a young Barry Sanders make.

They pitched the ball out to him going left, he was going outside, stopped and dipped a shoulder, the Buc out there took the fake, and boom, that quick, Walter was around the corner outside. Unbelievable.

It was the kind of running play that could only have been Walter Payton. He looked like a Royal Lipizzan stallion out there, doing his stuff—with those high-leg kicks, running stiff-legged.

You know, I don't think he would do that to show off. When you've got fluid on your knees, you run stiff like that. He never said anything to anybody about it, but I knew because when I was in the training room getting my knee drained, he'd be there standing in line.

We had another couple of interceptions that day, which goes to show you what pressure can mean. Sacks and interceptions are byproducts of the pressure you get.

If you're getting back there and the quarterback is throwing off his back foot, that pass doesn't have much zip on it and the cornerback can break.

Oh, yeah. This was our rematch against James Wilder, and you better believe Buddy made him our special emphasis.

After that first game, only one running back all season had a 100-yard game against us, and that was Gerald Riggs in Atlanta, who carried it 30 times in a game we won 36-0.

The Bucs knew we were going to stop Wilder. They threw the ball a bunch, and it made sense. When you play a team twice a year, and the first time they run the ball like they did, I promise you Tampa Bay's offensive coordinator knew we were going to put emphasis on shutting that shit down the second time.

So they went away from Wilder, who only ran it 18 times for 29 yards. On the other hand, Steve DeBerg threw for 346 yards. Not that it mattered.

GAME 6: BEARS 26, SAN FRANCISCO 10
October 13, Candlestick Park

Did I say we weren't getting a lot of attention? Not after this one.

I'd like to say it was because I had one of the best games of my career, which I did. But it wasn't.

This game was big for a lot of reasons. Walter started a streak of what became a record nine straight games with at least 100 rushing yards. We sacked Montana seven times. We got payback for the NFC championship.

And out of that payback, the darling of the media, William "the Refrigerator" Perry, was born. But I'll get to that in a minute.

I always loved it when we'd go to somebody else's house and hand it to them, just like with the Redskins. And we really wanted to do the same thing against the 49ers in Candlestick.

Once we did, I knew we were going to the Super Bowl. We'd just beaten the defending Super Bowl champions in their house, with no excuses. They were there in all their glory—Montana, Jerry Rice, Roger Craig—nobody on their team was hurt, they couldn't bitch they had jet lag because we were in their stadium, and we handed it to 'em.

Before the game, I walked up to Jim McMahon and said, "You get us an early lead, we're going to win this game."

First possession, he went out there and drove us 73 yards in six plays for a touchdown. McMahon came back to the sideline, looked at me and said, "Was that quick enough, Steve?"

We scored three out of the first four times we had the ball and were winning 16-0. Their only touchdown came on an interception return.

All day, I went against their All-Pro guard, Randy Cross, and Keith Farnhorst, a tackle. It wasn't a lot of fun, because they weren't exactly the Marquis of Queensbury—in fact, the 49ers were the worst team I played against as far as high-low blocking you.

The only thing I'd do where I was kind of askew of the rules was I had this pass rush where I'd fade outside to get the guy leaning over thinking that's where I'm going, then I'd slap the shit out of his inside shoulder. Sometimes that slap would ride up and hit him in the ear hole. Of course, the head-slap was the thing Deacon Jones used to get to do legally that they outlawed.

Even with those devious double-teams, I actually had the 49ers' plan down so much, I was having one of those Singletary days where I knew what was coming. One play started and I knew it was going to be a screen to Roger Craig out in the right flat. The ball was snapped; I didn't rush Montana. I started shuffling down the line to my right to get in the middle of the screen. I was out there so fast, he had to try to lob the ball over me. I jumped, almost intercepted it, tipped it and got a pass defended.

I also sacked him, for once had a great day against the pox on my career, and got a game ball.

Eventually, we all got our sweetest revenge for the NFC championship game. All week, Ditka was motivating us, reminding us how they'd used Guy McIntyre to run out the clock.

He's saying, "They not only beat our ass, but they rubbed it in running out the clock with a guard in the backfield."

It was good motivation, but putting a guard as your lead block in short yardage is kind of smart. Why have a small full-back when you can have an offensive guard leading in the hole? And Bill Walsh was an offensive genius.

But even a genius can do things that will hype up the other team.

So we were up 26-10 at the end of the game, running out the clock. Ditka trotted out William Perry, baby.

Walsh didn't give the ball to Guy McIntyre. But to one-up that, Ditka handed the ball off to William. They stacked him up at the line, he didn't get any yards, but the legend was born.

We all loved it. We were yelling and screaming in the locker room, but none of us knew it was going to take off to the tune of him making like $6 million in endorsements after the season's over—hell, it started before the season was over.

One of the first things Fridge did was a McDonald's commercial during the season—with me, Dan and Dave Duerson. We're all sitting at the table eating our cheeseburgers and Fridge is like the comic relief.

GAME 7: BEARS 23, GREEN BAY 7
October 21, Soldier Field

OK, it's not like Mike Ditka and Forrest Gregg were buddies before this.

I remember in '84, in the preseason, when I was out with that hurt knee, we played Green Bay in Milwaukee, where both teams had to stand on the same sideline. I was in a hospital bed with my leg up watching it on TV, and I could see during the game the two coaches cussing at each other on the same sideline. I was just waiting for the first punch.

But, my God, this turned into a war—and they were Patton and Rommel while we were tanks.

It was *Monday Night Football*, we were a week after the Fridge's debut on offense, and Ditka didn't bother waiting until we were running out the clock to bring him in.

I'm not saying there wasn't a legitimate football reason to do it. Practicing with William, Ditka realized what a juggernaut he was in the backfield.

Remember how Walter always had to jump over the pile in short yardage? Well, in this game, William being the lead fullback blocking, Walter walked in for our first score.

You could see in the film, there was this big pile of Packers on the goal line, and when William hit into them, they moved back. George Cumby took a direct shot and went backward like a car hit him.

Then William scored our second touchdown, and there was no denying he was a phenomenon. You'd better believe he only got the chance to score because it was the Green Bay Packers and Forrest Gregg.

Even our punter, Maury Buford, threw a pass that day. We were pulling out all stops.

It was amazing, the way Mike Ditka came through his football career just absolutely hating the Green Bay Packers. You could see the ramifications of it every time you looked at a game plan for the Packers.

I promise you, if you had been watching Mike Ditka after that first touchdown by the Fridge, you'd have seen him thumbing his nose at Forrest Gregg.

The rest of us? We couldn't help laughing.

Everything that came out of the Fridge kind of tickled your funnybone. The fat guy scoring the touchdown; the cheerleaders he had, the Refrigerettes, none of 'em being under 200 pounds; it was all comical. We all loved it.

GAME 8: BEARS 27, VIKINGS 9
October 27, Soldier Field

We were at the halfway point now, and this, I think, was where we really started rolling.

After we beat Green Bay on *Monday Night* and our fat guy scored, everybody wanted to know about the Bears.

The media could always come into the locker room during our lunch hour, and the first day back after Monday, there was more media in the locker room than football players. And it wasn't just media from around Chicago; they were from everywhere.

But you'd better believe we were ready for it.

There's a saying I've heard, "When you take the characters out of the game, you take the character out of the game." Our team was chock-full of characters in their own right. Every guy was a freaking sound bite for any media who wanted to talk to him. It wasn't like you had to fabricate something to make it more colorful—it was just verbatim what one guy said making an article.

You might run into a team nowadays that has a couple of guys who are good sound bites, but our team was full of them. Hell, you just had to follow McMahon around—you didn't even have to ask him a question.

Anyway, the Vikings were one of the teams I always played well against. And they were always the worst team I can recall in terms of being front-runners. They're hell on wheels when they've got a lead, but you get up on them, they'll quit before anybody else.

We got up on them 10-0 that day, and the rest was a jail-break. Even Fridge, feeding the legend, got his first sack. We got four all day, to go with five interceptions, while Kramer and Wade Wilson went 21 of 46 between 'em.

GAME 9: BEARS 16, GREEN BAY 10
November 3, Lambeau Field

This game just furthered the legend of William Perry, who caught his first touchdown pass. Beautiful. What a way to foster hate in an arch-rivalry. How much more can you rub it in?

But it's still Green Bay, and no matter how bad they are, they're still gonna play us tough. Actually, they played us dirty. This was the game one of their DBs, Mark Lee, took Walter way out of bounds and over a bench on the sideline, and Kenny Stills got ejected for a really late hit on Matt Suhey.

In the fourth quarter, we were losing 10-7, but for whatever reason they got back by their end zone and I could see by the way the offensive linemen were sitting back, they were going to throw a pass.

When both Walter and Jim were clicking, we were pretty hard to beat. (Photo by **Daily Southtown; Tinley Park, Illinois)**

So I got up in my track running stance, and it was so loud, when the ball was snapped, the guard got off later than I did. I ran around outside him, hardly touched, and I got back to the quarterback before he got back to set up.

I got back and sacked Jim Zorn for a safety.

That made it 10-9, and they had to punt the ball to us from the 20-yard line. We got the ball on their 49, Ditka handed the ball off to Walter three times—Walter had 192 yards that day, his best game of the year—Walter scored on a 27-yard run, and we won.

GAME 10: BEARS 24, DETROIT 10
November 10, Soldier Field

At this stage of the year, the defense finally really had its shit together.

This game was a classic example of how you get to be the No. 1 defense. It doesn't have to do with points. It's the yardage you give up rushing and passing. We held the Lions to 106 yards of total offense. With Walter and Matt Suhey both running for over 100 yards, we held the ball for over 41 minutes to not quite 19 for them.

Steve Fuller played that day and for the next couple of games. That was fairly typical of what happened most years in Jim McMahon's career, except most years he was hurt and couldn't play in the playoffs.

Like I said, that's a major contributing factor to why we didn't win another couple Super Bowls. We were playing in the playoffs with Doug Flutie, Steve Fuller and Mike Tomczak instead of Jim McMahon.

But playing with a second-string quarterback didn't stop us from dominating, not against the Lions.

GAME 11: BEARS 44, DALLAS 0
November 17, Texas Stadium

The turning point, baby. This was a good Dallas team, not some red-headed stepchild. They had Tony Dorsett, Danny White, Randy White, Too Tall Jones, the Doomsday Defense, all that BS.

They were talking a little bit before the game, too. One of their corners, Everson Walls, said something like, "They're 10-0, but they ain't played nobody yet."

Hah!

After we beat 'em 44-0, Dan Hampton told all the reporters, "You know, Everson Walls was right. We still ain't played nobody."

That was one of those days we could've beaten them 3-0. Right out of the box, we crushed them on defense, a ball got knocked up, Richard Dent grabbed it and scored a touchdown. They weren't gonna do nothin'.

It was the worst defeat in Cowboy history. It was so bad, their running back, Tony Dorsett, was taking snaps right before halftime after we knocked out Danny White.

Remember, I'm from Texas, and football is a religion down there. I've never heard a quieter stadium in the state of Texas during a football game, and I never will.

One thing I regret from the game was I cussed one of my heroes. In college, we ran the flex defense like the Cowboys, so I watched hours of tape on Randy White.

I saw him quit in the third quarter, and it crushed me.

We were all about the shutout, so even when it was 44-0, the starters were still in there. And Tony Dorsett was still in there, because I guess he had incentives and wanted to lead the league in rushing or something.

So in the third quarter, we ran Tony out of bounds on their side. There was Tom Landry standing right next to me, and behind him was Randy White, and he already had his baseball hat on, he was through for the day. I couldn't hold it back.

I said, "Randy, I've always looked up to your fuckin' ass, but look at you over here. I don't care if the score's a hundred to nothin', I'd never quit. You pussy."

Right in front of Landry.

Randy still hates me, and I'd like to apologize. It was just something I said in the heat of the battle.

Anyway, we were 11-0 now. We clinched the division and the playoffs earlier than anybody else in a 16-game schedule ever had.

We were on a "going to the Super Bowl" roll now and getting pretty cocky, too. In fact, I started doing something I got from Dick Butkus, reading his book in junior high.

You know how in pregame warm ups, after everyone warms up with their position, everybody comes together and the offense runs plays against the defense?

I stopped doing that. I'd go stand at the 50-yard line and stare at the other team.

Talking about it later, I found out other teams got out of it exactly what I wanted them to. Some guy on another team would say, "Yeah, we used to see y'all standing there staring at us like crazy motherfuckers."

Nice to know it had the desired effect.

GAME 12: BEARS 36, ATLANTA 0
November 24, Soldier Field

Like I said, we were on a roll now, baby. Second straight shutout, Walter's seventh straight 100-yard game. For Pete's sake, Henry Waechter got three sacks.

Oh boy, we're going to Miami and we're going to kick some ass.

Of course, that attitude can come back to bite you on the ass—and I'm glad it did. Miami was the wakeup call we needed so we didn't go into the playoffs and get our asses beat before going to the Super Bowl.

GAME 13: MIAMI 35, BEARS 24
December 2, Orange Bowl

The whole week leading up to this game, all we heard was, "You guys are the greatest ever. What are you going to do next? What do y'all got in store for us as you go undefeated through the Super Bowl?"

Ditka was more up on this stuff than we were, because at the time we were about to become the youngest team ever to go to a Super Bowl. We thought we were going back every year.

Ditka knew what we cost ourselves when we went down there and fucked up our undefeated year. Of course, the Dolphins knew it, too, because they called in all markers to try to keep their undefeated season protected. Every old Dolphin they could find was in the stadium for that game. They knew how good we were—that's why they were there.

One reason we got beat was McMahon didn't start. Another was that on the Dolphins' first five possessions, they scored five times.

We should have known it wasn't our night when one of Dan Marino's first touchdown passes bounced off Hampton's helmet. A ball bouncing off a helmet is supposed to die, but this one somehow flew farther, like a rock skipping off a lake. Nat Moore was behind the coverage, the ball went right into his hands, and he got a 33-yard touchdown.

At halftime, Buddy Ryan and Mike Ditka had to be pulled apart before they started throwing punches.

With five possessions, five scores, you better believe Ditka was wanting to know what was going on. Walking into the locker room, he was on Buddy's ass. That chapped Buddy good, and he'd be the first one to throw a punch at you—as Kevin Gilbride found out a few years later in Arizona. Don't question what Buddy's doing.

So the argument started on the way to the locker room. Once they got in, they were in each other's faces. The guys on the team had to separate them—the offense getting Ditka away from Ryan and defensive guys holding Buddy.

It didn't exactly bode well for the second half.

But then, I don't know what we could have done. It was sort of like any golfer, any pool player, I don't care how good you are, how consistent, there's gonna be that day you miss that two-foot putt with the game on the line, or there's the eight ball, right in the pocket, you can't miss, and somehow it doesn't go in.

Plus, every year, it was like a curse. We'd have two *Monday Night* games a year because we were a good team. One, we'd be great, the other, we'd get our asses blown out. Every year. I don't know what it was about. There was a curse. Somebody had a Bears kewpie doll and it was full of needles one Monday a year.

There was no doubt in my mind, if we'd have played the Dolphins at 12 o'clock on a Sunday, we'd have beat the shit out of them. I was so sure at the time that, when the Miami Dolphins were playing in the AFC championship game, I was rooting for them. I wanted some justice.

And like I said, we were more than a little full of ourselves.

Being 12-0, we were already in the playoffs. We got down to Miami, and I tell you, I don't know how the Dolphins or the Tampa Bay Bucs can ever field a winning team. You're down in the tropics where everbody goes to vacation. Every time we had a game in Florida, some Bears fans were going, too—and the Sunday night before that Miami game, I think I saw just about all of them out somewhere.

I think we started out at Hooters and it just degenerated from there. We were thinking, "We've got plenty of time to recover. It's not a 12 o'clock game, we don't play 'til late."

THE SUPER BOWL SHUFFLE

Sorry, I've got to take a timeout from the game by game to get something off my chest—the goddamn "Super Bowl Shuffle."

I was pissed off about this from the inception until—well, I'm still mad about it.

Everybody had known for a couple of weeks that, on Tuesday after we got back from Miami, the guys were going to start shooting the "Super Bowl Shuffle." If you don't remember, it was a music video about how we were going to the Super Bowl. Nobody's team had done one before, and I didn't think we should.

I could see it if we'd been there the year before and lost, saying, "We're going to go back and win it this time." But we didn't even get close. We got out asses run out of the stadium by 'Frisco in the NFC championship game in '84.

My opinion, how often do things work out for you when you brag about doing them before the fact? Hardly ever. I thought the sumbitches had jinxed us.

I wasn't happy about it; neither was Hampton. Talk about bulletin board material. Any coach who wants to get his team fired up to play against the Bears in the playoffs or the Super Bowl, all he's got to do is put that fucking thing on the night before the game.

But the thing that really chapped my ass was, after the loss, I couldn't believe they were still going to do it. I actually assumed it wasn't going to be done. I was mistaken.

We got into Chicago about 3 a.m. These guys were going to start filming at 7 a.m.

So after they got their asses beat, they had to go on no sleep to some studio and start shuffling about how they're going to the Super Bowl.

Gary Fencik shouldn't have done it, because he showed everybody how horseshit of a dancer he was. And Steve Fuller, everybody knew he was bluegrass, redneck country when he opened his mouth.

Anyway, I don't think it worked out quite the way the guys who did it expected. They got paid five grand apiece for it; the rest of the money was supposed to go to charity, but after it became a gold record and was up for a Grammy, they found out most of the money didn't go where they thought it would.

Anybody who reads this book, please, know one reason why I'm so pissed off about it: When I do appearances to this day, people come up to me and say, "Weren't you in the 'Super Bowl Shuffle?'" I've got a Super Bowl ring on, and the thing they remember is that "Super Bowl Shuffle." I go to appearances, and they're playing that song like it's the Bears fight song or something.

I loathe it.

And now, back to the season.

GAME 14: BEARS 17, INDIANAPOLIS 10
December 8, Soldier Field

It was a close game. I think we were all playing tight because of the Miami loss.

Still, the game wasn't as close as the score. We dominated them. They had a long score late.

But we did maybe play a little close to the vest. Most big plays—and we were nothing if not a big-play defense—are made after a guy takes care of his responsibility, then goes outside of that and makes the play.

After you get your ass handed to you, guys are about making sure they're taking care of their responsibilities—so those big plays don't happen.

GAME 15: BEARS 19, NEW YORK JETS 6
December 14, Giants Stadium

The Jets were a good team. They made the playoffs that year, and Ken O'Brien, their quarterback, was the league's top-rated passer when we played them.

They had 122 yards passing that day, 89 after you subtract the lost yardage from four sacks.

The first thing you've got to do is predicate every game plan on the best thing your opponent does. They're going to get to it sometime during the game. You just hope they can't do anything else.

It's like with John Elway. He goes to two Super Bowls and loses, but he gets Terrell Davis behind him and they win two.

Now, you can't just stop Elway. You've got to stop Davis, too. And because you've got to stop Davis, it opens up for John Elway.

The only bad thing from the game was it instigated my fourth knee operation.

It was a cold game, so the Astrotruf was frozen. Another jailbreak, we went after O'Brien, somebody wiped him out before I could get to him. The first thing that hit was my knee on the turf, and I tore cartilage.

Every week from then on, until I got it operated on after the Super Bowl, I had to have it drained.

GAME 16: BEARS 37, DETROIT 17
December 22, Pontiac Silverdome

The one thing I'll never forget about this game—mostly because they're still showing it on highlights—is Wilber Marshall hitting Joe Ferguson and just knocking him out.

You could tell, just like a boxing match where a guy's been hit so hard he's already out before he hit the ground, Joe was out like a light.

Remember in the old days, how they'd pick a guy's arm up and if it flopped down, he's out? Richard Dent walked up to Joe, picked his arm up, let it go and it just flopped back to the ground. I shouldn't have been laughing about it, but I was.

The play itself was a thing of beauty. Joe took the snap in a passing situation, and here we came. Wilber was actually in the flat in coverage, not even rushing, but because we flushed Joe out to my right toward Wilber, Wilber's job was to come up and force the play.

Joe saw him coming, and he got the pass off, just dumping it somewhere. But he had to straighten up, turning to his right, to throw the ball, because he was right-handed.

You've got to understand how fast Wilber Marshall was. If the perception is he was linebacker fast, that's wrong. He was defensive back fast—and that's what cost Joe Ferguson. He thought he had time to square up and get rid of the ball before Wilber got there, but Wilber hit him right in the mouth with his helmet.

Wilber didn't even have to dive. Most great shots, the guy lays out like a missile, hits his target and goes down with him. But Wilber just ran up and boom! Then he was standing there while Joe goes out.

Now we were on to the playoffs, and we didn't care at all that we lost to Miami. We thought because we were a young team we had plenty of time to have an undefeated season and go back to the Super Bowl.

Chapter 6

BEAR WEATHER: THE 1985 PLAYOFFS

THE WINDY, COLD CITY

I don't know how it came as a surprise to anybody, except maybe that it had been so long since there was an NFL playoff game in Chicago—1963 to be exact. But this was January. This was Soldier Field, right on Lake Michigan, back in the days when the columns were taller than the stands.

It was cold, and it was windy, and those things became a prevailing factor in our playoff games. Hell, they were a factor most games, considering it seemed like nobody but Kevin Butler could kick in Soldier Field. Every other kicker and most quarterbacks who came in would have something to say about the wind gusts, and the later in winter it got, the worse it got.

At least we were acclimated to it. It didn't bother us as much. Like the Denver Broncos playing up in that thin air at Mile High Stadium.

We knew the teams coming in there, it bothered the shit out of them, especially the teams from warm-weather cities.

We wanted a rematch with Miami in the Super Bowl. (Photo by Daily Southtown; *Tinley Park, Illinois)*

LIKING OUR CHANCES

I knew we were just one play away from McMahon getting hurt. But as long as McMahon stayed healthy, we were pretty confident—really on the side of arrogant. We felt like nobody could beat us, and if they did it was a fluke.

To us, the Miami Dolphins were the clear No. 2 team, our main challenger. I couldn't wait for them to win the AFC championship and meet us in the Super Bowl so we could rectify that one defeat. I know most people don't think that way; they'd be scared to play them in the Super Bowl because they beat us. They'd want to play someone else.

Cowards.

DOING FOR RICHARD

So we got the regular season out of the way and were rolling into the playoffs. All of a sudden, Richard Dent and his agent came up in the press and said they weren't going to play unless they got a new contract.

Seems like their reasoning was the year's over, he doesn't have a contract, he's not going to play. Something like that. Or maybe it was he wasn't going to play the next year.

Either way, in my mind, that didn't make sense, so we set it up in practice to turn him loose, to set him free in the game, make him the Defensive MVP so the Bears would have to deal with him.

We set up this line stunt called the Echo, where Dan and I slanted to the right toward Richard, and he came around both of us, to the outside of me. The guard blocked me, I held the center, and the tackle was out blocking on Mike Hartenstine or whoever the defensive end was, and Richard would come in that gap.

It seems like a long way to go, and the way they run those games now in pro football, it is. They almost never run three-man games, because there's no time, and even when they run a two-man game it takes too long because the second guy coming around is rounding it off instead of running on an angle to the quarterback, because the first guy is just stopping his man at the line of scrimmage.

You want to penetrate, like a fullback blocking on a run.

Now, what we were doing wouldn't work so well with the West Coast offense and quick drops. But back then, the seven-step drop was still in vogue. It worked.

We set Richard free about three times and he was knocking the shit out of Phil Simms all the time. He ended up with three and a half of our six sacks that day.

It just happened that that game, the Echo was tailor-made for what they were trying to do, and we didn't even realize it when we were thinking about running it. But after we ran it the first time, I knew it was going to work whenever I saw they were going to drop back to pass.

It was called at the line of scrimmage, and the first time I called it, it was a long-yardage play. With that long-yardage play, we had the chance for this Echo to get home because Simms was going to seven-step drop. It came clean, real fast, too. It happened quick. For the rest of the game, I knew their game plan was going to be to try to bust a long play on our defense. Because we blitzed a lot, there was a chance to get a long, successful play—but that takes time.

Richard knew. I told him. I said, "We're going to make you a hero." In the fourth quarter, we'd already beat them, but we stayed in there because we wanted to shut them out.

Richard was looking down the line of scrimmage, actually trying to call it out himself before I could read what the offensive line was going to do. You had to see if it was going to be a pass. You had to see by the strength of the formation whether they were going to east or west block it.

I'd have to basically wave him off—just wait a second, Richard. And he's "more, more, more." Like a little kid.

It wasn't like we were taking a chance of losing the game for Richard. A few plays out of every game wasn't a big deal. Dan was still outside where Richard was supposed to be in containment, so we weren't fucking the defense to help Richard. The jobs were all covered, just switched.

We went through the whole playoffs set up like that. Richard was the Super Bowl MVP and he got his money.

FEEL THE BREEZE

Poor Sean Landetta. The guy stayed in the NFL longer than just about anybody this side of George Blanda, and he's still remembered mostly for whiffing on a punt.

Being an old kicker myself, I have some sympathy—but how Landetta punts the ball is not conducive to punting in high gusts of wind. Some punters cradle the ball on their hand; others grab the tip of the ball—Landetta cradled it.

Having hold of the ball is the best way to punt when you're dealing with the wind. The way Landetta did it, you actually have to get your hand out of the way before you punt the ball, so it's suspended in midair, and if there's a gust of wind it blows it. That's what happened to him. The wind turned the nose of the ball before he could punt it, moved it out of his way.

Shawn Gayle picked it up and ran it in from five yards out for our first score. That was the first big play he made in his career—and he went on to become All-Pro.

WAIT TILL NEXT YEAR

Even though we ended up winning, you could see the Giants had a good defense—and it turned out to be a great defense, because they won the Super Bowl the next year.

I think our game turned out to be their Waterloo like we had with the 49ers the year before. They realized how that felt and that they hadn't raised their goals or their expectations high enough. They were happy just to be where they were, and they got their asses whipped for it.

One thing's for sure, though, Jimbo Covert completely took Lawrence Taylor out of his game that day. Shut his ass down.

Not too many people realize what the worth of the offensive line is. I promise you Lawrence Taylor was trying to be the MVP himself, but Covert shut him down. There's one clip in the official '85 highlight film that shows Covert just splattering Taylor, boom, flat on his back.

Just goes to show you Covert was the best offensive lineman in the league, before his back got hurt. If he'd had a long career, he'd be in the Hall of Fame no question, just like Taylor is.

FEVER PITCH

In some ways, it was just another Bears win that year—we held them to 32 yards rushing, got a bunch of sacks and held the ball most of the day.

But if you're talking about the fan fervor, it kicked up another step higher, which was natural seeing as there hadn't been a Bears playoff game in Chicago since the 1963 championship game.

I always stayed in the locker room a long time after games— so long that whoever was there from my family would be mad at me for making them stand around. After we beat the Giants, I took my time as usual, but the mob of people, the fans, were still there waiting to get a glimpse. Not standing around inside the stadium, but outside. They were almost groupies.

You know how you hear the buzz above the din? That buzz was all over town. Like electricity.

It was a distraction. Everybody was looking for their piece. Media, fans, even people who weren't fans—imagine that, there's lots of people in Chicago who aren't Bears fans.

Everybody wanted a piece, and for the most part we were pretty happy to accommodate them. That was when we started coming into our own about being flamboyant personalities and characters, finding out that sells.

BULLETIN BOARD MATERIAL

Going into the Rams game, Buddy Ryan kind of pissed me off.

It wasn't like the "Super Bowl Shuffle" was enough motivation for anybody we were going to play to get into the Super Bowl. He had to go challenge the leading rusher in the league.

Buddy said, "We're going to make Eric Dickerson fumble three times." God, you don't know how that irritated me.

I mean, Ditka would do it on occasion—like the time a couple of years later everybody in Minnesota raised a fuss when he called the Vikings' stadium the Rollerdome. I believe they beat us that day, but anyway...

Buddy was cocky and arrogant and he said we were going to make Dickerson fumble three times and win the game. I don't know for sure why he said it, but I blame it on the media gigging him.

You know how it is. You keep asking the question until you get the answer you want. They were probably telling him, "Eric

Dickerson, the rushing champion of the league, how can you possibly stop him? Nobody can stop him." I can just hear Buddy saying, "Ah, we're going to make him fumble three times and shut his ass down, that's how."

Buddy was not far from wrong, though. Dickerson fumbled twice and we shut his ass down. He had 17 carries for 46 yards and on one short-yardage play, Mike Singletary met him head on, stood him up and pushed him back.

LET IT SNOW

The biggest play of the game, at least in terms of making you wonder if somebody up there in that press box in the sky was scripting the whole thing, came late.

We were already winning 17-0. We already know those L.A. boys were shivering in their boots, them with their long sleeves on and us with our bare arms acting like we don't feel a thing.

Hell, in the highlight film from that game, one of their defensive linemen looks over at the camera and says, "Why the hell don't they put a dome over this thing?" And that's before the game. So you know the Rams were out of their element.

To tell you the truth, it was colder in the Giants game. But the wind was blowing harder for the Rams.

Anyway, the Rams were trying to make something happen. Their quarterback, Dieter Brock, dropped back. We sacked him, he fumbled, Wilber picked it up.

And in the middle of his 52-yard runback for a touchdown, it started snowing.

Bear weather. A sign from God that we're the chosen team.

At least, that's the way the fans reacted to it.

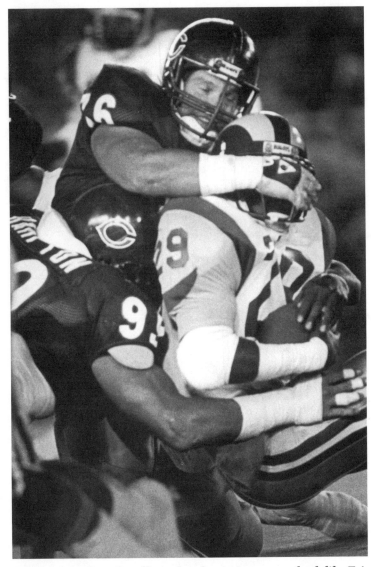

Regular season or playoffs, we loved stopping a great back like Eric Dickerson. (Photo by **Daily Southtown;** *Tinley Park, Illinois)*

Hey, I think it's all head games, and if that works in a positive sense, well, then I'm all about head games. It's all psychology, baby.

We were already winning the game 17-0. Maybe if we were losing the game 23-17 and that happened, I'd think God was shining down on us or something, but no. We won 24-0. We could've played 'em on the beach and won.

There was no big celebration. It was understated in the locker room after the game. We remembered the feeling of the year before, going into the locker room with our asses handed to us.

We were in it to win the Super Bowl, not to get there. Hell, we were in it to win the Super Bowl, then three-peat. We were pretty cocky.

Of course, we had reason.

Two playoff games, two shutouts. Bring on New Orleans.

Chapter 7

THE BIG EASY

HIGH ROLLERS

I'm not a gambler, but I do happen to know that after the conference championships, we were made 21-point favorites for Super Bowl XX in New Orleans.

But when the oddsmakers saw how much we were partying on Bourbon Street the week before the game, the spread went to 10.

HOMEBODY

We had two weeks between the conference championships and the game, so we spent the first in Georgia at the Falcons' training facility. It was just like a regular-season game week—practice and go home.

To me, it wasn't out of the ordinary, because back then I wasn't into the media hype and stuff I got into later in my career. After a while, I realized nobody knew who I was, so I'd better start talking about myself, but that first week I was just going home, staying to myself.

Well, more or less. It wasn't like I was a priest that week. We were young and brash and we were going to play in the Super Bowl every year as far as we were concerned. To slow down would be to become a hypocrite.

On the other hand, things clearly sped up in New Orleans.

LAISSEZ LES BONS TEMPS ROULER

You'd think a good old southern boy like me would've been out on Bourbon Street in New Orleans sometime in his life, right? Not until the Super Bowl, baby, and when I got there it was like all the cajuns say, "Laissez les bons temps rouler."

Let the good times roll.

Our last day in Lake Forest, we had a walk-through at Halas then got on a plane. When we got off the plane, we went straight to Bourbon Street—didn't even check into the hotel—and started partying.

Well, we went to the hotel on the team bus, but we were staying in the hotel attached to the Superdome, and that's walking distance to Bourbon Street, so right out of the box we walked over and started drinking.

Actually, I think we were already drunk when we got off the plane.

Back then, Hampton and I would carry around a liter of Crown Royal in our bags. Really, we'd been doing it ever since we met.

It usually wasn't to drink going there, but to drink on the plane coming back from a game. We'd sit beside each other on the plane, have our little country & western music going, usually some Hank Williams Jr., and had our bottle to drink. Beer's fattening, you know, and I had a waistline back then.

In fact, it was our superstition to go have two Crown and 7s in the hotel bar the night before a game. Something for the effort, we called it.

As you get older, some of those superstitions wear you down and you don't do them anymore. But this was the Super Bowl—and with plenty of time to rest up.

Bourbon Street was everything it was cracked up to be. Bars up and down the street for blocks, people walking down the middle with drinks in their hands. And we were basically VIPs—carte blanche everywhere.

That first Monday night, I fell victim like most tourists do to the Hurricanes at Pat O'Brien's. It's this big old umbrella drink with about seven shots of different kinds of booze in it—and when you walk in the place already drunk, one of them is going to put you over the edge.

So that Monday night, I left a little dissolved Hurricane juice in the alley behind Pat O'Brien's.

But it helps when you're a finely tuned athlete. Your body recovers in a few hours and you're able to drink again.

AWAY FROM THE ACTION

I don't want you to get the impression we went out and partied every second of every night we were in New Orleans. That second night after practice we went over to a hospital to visit kids in the terminal children's ward.

That's tough to do. Always has been. Holy Christ, that'll put everything in perspective.

How do you go in there? I mean, what do you say when you first meet somebody? "How are you doing?" I know the answer. They're dying.

What do you say to a little kid like that? I'd say things like, "Everybody looks up to me, but I'm looking up to you because you're going to be in heaven before me. You're going to be on God's football team, all practiced up and ready to whip my butt when I get up there."

Half the little kids didn't know who we were. All the parents did, all the hospital staff did. It was like more of an appearance for them than for the kids, from what I saw. But I might've pissed a few of them off, because I was there for the kids.

Just the sheer presence of huge individuals sometimes is enough to make a kid smile, so at least I could do that. That's what I think wrestling is all about, just these cartoon characters that wrestling fans look at like, "Wow."

FAMILY MATTERS

My mother tells the story of me taking her and the family—I had 30 family members there—out the first night they were in.

I think it was Thursday. The next night, getting closer to the game, I didn't go out with them. But this night, free drinks, free food, no standing in line. The next night, they don't go out with me, they're back at the end of the line with everybody else.

Actually, that first night, she might not have minded being left outside the first bar we went to. In those first few nights drinking, I hadn't been all the way down the end of the street yet, so I said, "Let's start all the way down the end and work our way up front."

Well, we found out the first bar was a gay bar, with transvestites in it. Wasn't too long before my mother wanted to get out of there. Didn't bother me. Shoot, they're fans, too.

Something did bother me relating to family during the week, though. In one of the team meetings, Ditka came in and told us that after the Super Bowl, the Bears were going to have a party in the ballroom of the hotel if we win, and we'd all get 20 tickets to the party.

Now every player had gotten 30 Super Bowl game tickets each. I stood up and said, "Well, Mike, what 10 family members do you want me to tell they aren't important enough to me to come to this fuckin' party?"

He figured I was talking for the whole team, which I was, really, and said, "You young fuckers haven't been to a Super Bowl, you don't know what it's like, you don't know the privileges and how you should be treated." Basically, he was saying, "Suck on it. The McCaskeys are screwing you out of the 10 people you had coming." And we found out later the sumbitches closed the party down at 10:30.

It was no time after the game. The party was over in a couple hours. That's chicken shit. That's why I believe that story you hear about George Halas to his daughter on his death bed:

"Please, Virginia, anybody but Michael."

AND ANOTHER STORY I BELIEVE...

Pretty famously, Jim McMahon got in trouble during Super Bowl week for supposedly telling a radio reporter that all the women of New Orleans were sluts and the men were nuts.

OK, so he never actually said it. At least not to a radio reporter.

But let me tell you, I understand the impression.

When you go out and every minute there's some groupie wanting to give you a piece of ass, and you're in New Orleans—even if they're not from New Orleans, what's your impression going to be?

I tell you what it is:

"Every woman I met in New Orleans was a slut."

McMahon (here ignoring Vince Tobin later in his career) got himself into some trouble during the Super Bowl week. (Photo by **Daily Southtown***; Tinley Park, Illinois)*

Even if McMahon never said it, women ain't going down on Bourbon Street to try to become nuns. They're there to get theirs. Even if it didn't happen, I could see McMahon saying it, because that was my perception.

You can go down there the deadest time of the year, and you'll still have guys down there with beads wanting girls to show them their titties. Boy, I didn't even have to have beads back then. Things were getting thrown at me I didn't even want.

Anyway, people were wondering if it was going to be a distraction. Come on.

It was hilarious. It was entertaining.

IT'S MY PARTY

When I went out during the week, it was with the night riders—me, Hampton, Mike Hartenstine and Henry Waechter. But that didn't mean we didn't see our teammates.

We'd be walking down the street and somebody would say, "Hey, so-and-so's in there." So we'd go in. Every bar along the street, it was like a different Bear was having a personal appearance, or at least different cliques of Bears. It was like a block party—our block party.

It damn sure wasn't the Patriots' party. You'd see their fans here and there, but they were getting squelched. They were getting freight-trained.

THE SATURDAY SERMON

One thing people always want to know when I'm out making appearances is what Ditka told us the night before the Super Bowl, what fiery oratory he used to stir our passions.

This is usually where I tell them a joke about Ditka's speaking prowess, but since it calls into question the sexual preference of our quarterback, I think I'll let it be. After using it so many times, I'm getting tired of telling that joke, anyway.

To tell you the truth, Ditka was calm that night. The total opposite of what people think he's about.

People think he's about boiling up, cussing, and ranting and raving on the sidelines.

He just told us, "This is hype, it's another level, but don't let yourself go there, because then you're playing out of your norm. That's when guys start making mistakes and start forgetting what you're supposed to do. That's the first thing that beats you. That's when you see a big play happen."

He was just trying to keep us on an even keel, knowing that we were about to blow up.

OF BUDDY, GOOD-BYES AND CHALKBOARDS

The story was around all that week that the Philadelphia Eagles wanted Buddy Ryan to be their head coach.

Of course, we knew all along that it was not only the Philadelphia Eagles, but most every team that needed a head coach. Buddy Ryan was on their hit list. But during that two-week span before the Super Bowl, it was apparent that the Philadelphia Eagles were going to be on the forefront. Even so, it was all kept quiet, because it's disruptive to the team if they find out their defensive coordinator is leaving before the game.

I know, it's hard to believe that would be disruptive considering the way sports are covered and rumors are spread. You'd think we'd be used to it. But never underestimate the ability of an NFL jock to be stupid.

We know how much truth is in most press coverage—if you see something in the media saying this is the way it is, it ain't always that way. So as long as Buddy was with us, he was with us. He's on our side, he wouldn't be talking to the enemy—right?

But he did.

The night before the Super Bowl, after Ditka gave us his pep talk, we split off into offensive and defensive meetings. It's the same before any game, really, a meeting to find out, in the 13th hour, if everybody knows their job responsibility. Buddy and Vince Tobin, who came to be the defensive coordinator after him, both would give us a handwritten test on our responsibilities in whatever defense was going to be called.

At least, that's what we'd usually go over in these meetings, but that ain't what happened the night before the Super Bowl.

Buddy Ryan normally would get up, talk about what he wanted to talk about, then leave the meeting. He'd leave it up to Dale Haupt, our defensive line coach, to run the projector while we watched some more film on the other team.

Everything was going down the way it always had until Buddy got to the end of his talk. I can't even remember now what he'd said to that point, but I'll never forget the last thing he said, with tears in his eyes:

"Guys, no matter what happens, you guys will always be my heroes."

I knew he was gone right there.

He walked out of the room. It pissed me off so much, I couldn't sit there in my rage. I jumped up, grabbed the chair I was sitting in—a metal chair—and there was a chalkboard up in the front of the room, which I was pretty close to. I wasn't one of those guys sitting in the back. I grabbed my chair, and to sound off as loud as I could about my angst about this, I grabbed my chair and threw it at the blackboard, thinking it was just going to shatter.

I threw that chair and somehow it had the right spin so that all four legs hit the blackboard first, went through and stuck there. Hampton saw that, jumped up from his chair by the projector, smashed his big club of a hand into the projector and just destroyed it.

The offense was sitting across the ballroom, on the other side of one of those sliding divider things. They heard all this commotion.

The whole defense sounded like "Rarh!" like you hear fans in the stadium when the team walks out. The offense heard "Boom! Crash! Rarh!" then saw us all filing out of the meeting.

They talk shit to us to this day about how we got to get out of the meeting first. 'Cuz you know we all went back to our rooms and had milk and cookies and went to sleep.

ALONE WITH MY THOUGHTS

I always had this superstition involving coming out a couple of hours before anybody came out even for warm ups before a game, already in my cleats and football pants but not my shoulder pads and my helmet, to just walk around the field, stretch and get in the necessary state of mind.

It was no different for the Super Bowl, except for the fact that it was the Super Bowl, which made everything different.

At first, I was a little distracted by the stadium. I don't know why the NFL doesn't do it all the time, maybe it's too expensive or something, but it's impressive the way they get a Super Bowl stadium decorated up. It's just 10 times more pomp and circumstance than a regular-season game with the banners, the painting on the field and stuff. Little things count.

It didn't take long, though, before I was trying to get down to business. But in taking my usual walk, I kept running into some of the people I'd known in New England.

The equipment guy, the trainer, guys like that, were all trying to come up and talk to me. I fucked 'em all off, like, "Get the hell away from me, fucker." Vicious. Looking back, they were trying to acknowledge the Patriots were wrong about me, but I didn't even let them get the words out.

I sort of regret it now, but don't go up and screw with a predatory animal, you know?

SHUT OUT OF HISTORY

We shut out the Giants. We shut out the Rams.

If we'd have shut out the New England Patriots in the Super Bowl, we'd have pitched a shutout for the playoffs—no points—and that hasn't ever happened.

We were serious about it. Sure, we partied all week, but the business of football was attended to. There was not one mental mistake made in that game—by the defense.

Not that it mattered.

Walter Payton fumbled on the first series, which you can blame mostly on the offensive set being wrong.

In the huddle, they call the offensive set—which is where the tight end's supposed to be—and the backfield set with the play. They were called two different ways. The strength went one way and Walter went the other, opposite the blocking, and he got crushed.

Walter fumbled the ball, we stopped them right there, but it was so close they kicked the field goal. Three points, right at the beginning of the game. If that hadn't happened, we'd have shut them out, because it was a bunch of reserves who let Steve Grogan throw a touchdown pass at the end. No way we'd have let those guys on the field if we were working on a shutout.

A MOMENT OF DOUBT

After Walter Payton fumbled that ball, I had a little consternation, like, "Aw, shoot. They're going to be in the game with us."

It didn't last long.

New England beat Miami in the AFC championship by running the ball and keeping Dan Marino off the field. Against us, they decided to come out and try to trick us by throwing.

But I was always adept at reading offensive linemen by how they set whether it was going to be a run or a pass. When they come to the line of scrimmage with all five of them sitting back like they're taking a dump in the woods, it ain't going to be a run, baby.

Since I knew it was going to be a pass, I looked up at their starting quarterback, Tony Eason. Now, what does a quarterback usually do that gives away whether it's going to be a run or a pass? He looks down the field to see what the coverage is. But Tony Eason was wide-eyed, like a deer caught in the headlights, looking at our front four thinking, "Who's fixing to kill me when I drop back?"

That's when I knew we were going to win the game.

It ended up all three plays were passes, they completed one of them and ended up kicking the field goal.

THE EARLY KNOCKOUT

It was 3-0, we got the ball back and tied it with a field goal set up by a long pass to Willie Gault.

Then we traded punts; they got lousy field position. That's when they dropped back and neglected to double-team me. I beat their guard, Ron Wooten, and sacked Tony Eason. While I was in the process of taking him down, Richard Dent came in from the back and hit the ball. Eason fumbled, Dan Hampton recovered, we got another field goal and were up 6-3.

On the next series, they pitched the ball out to Craig James. Richard hit him, made him fumble, we get the ball back, again on their 13. Two snaps later, Matt Suhey scored on an 11-yard run.

That was big. If we'd have let them stay in the game, who knows? The longer you let that lesser team stay in the game, the more you build them up and there's a chance they're going to hang around until the end. You have to discourage them during the game, and a turnover deep in your own end, followed by a quick touchdown, is discouraging.

After that, the floodgates were open. It's like we were scoring every perceivable way. Reggie Phillips, a backup defensive back, had an interception return for a touchdown. Of course, the Fridge had to get in the act. It was just one of those games where it's your day, baby.

But then, it helped that the Patriots gave up after the first quarter. You could see it in their eyes and in their performance. They weren't on an emotional high; they were struggling.

HALF EMPTY

The Patriots had minus-19 yards of offense at halftime. My God, man. The reel of film, it's half-full. It was three-and-outs.

Our offense was controlling the ball and scoring. We went out, it wasn't just three-and-out, it was minus yards and out. I mean, minus-19 yards of total offense? It's amazing.

You'd think, winning 23-3 and rolling, we'd have been happy. We weren't. It was more like a frenzy. "More, more. Eat, eat." It was more of an adrenaline rush at halftime than it was before the game, and we were killing them.

We wanted to blow them out; 23-3 wasn't enough. Even for the coaches, considering they decided to run the punt return reverse that ended Les Frazier's career.

I mean, we're going to reverse-punt with a starting corner when the game's already blown out? That shows the fervor that was in the locker room at halftime.

Sure, the little special teams coach, Steve Kazor, was wanting to call it. But it was ultimately Mike Ditka's call. Ditka wanted to punctuate that victory with a blowout. What blew out was Les Frazier's knee.

I think Astroturf is more dangerous inside a dome. They don't crest the field in the middle for the water to run off like they do on an outdoor field. It's more conducive to hurting your knee when it's flat. When it's crested, your next step outside, toward the sideline, is kind of downhill. Both Les and New England's tight end, Lin Dawson, hurt their knees in that game without any real contact and were never the same.

GENEROUS TO A FAULT

After the third quarter, we were starting to get a little unfocused on the sidelines. Hell, I was high-fiving fans in the stands.

Maybe I should've stayed in the game. I gave up a chance to be the co-MVP with Richard Dent and a chance to be in the record book when I let my backup, Henry Waechter, go in.

I'd had some nice plays—the game's first sack, another they stole from me right before halftime where, three-man rush, I beat a double-team, swiped Grogan's legs, and he stumbled down, fixing to fall. Richard came along, fell on his back and got the sack.

To this day, most people tell me, "Ah, your Super Bowl, I quit watching it by halftime. I was bored." Well, so was I.

So I let Henry go in, Buddy ran a blitz when they dropped back in their end zone, Henry got a safety and a sack.

That safety is in the record books, that's what kills me. There have been other guys to get one, but is anybody ever going to get two safeties in a Super Bowl? Henry's always going to be in the record book. But I don't regret it or think I did wrong. By God, my teammate got some.

HEAVY CELEBRATING

During the game, Hampton and Otis told me they were carrying Buddy Ryan off the field. Dan told me and Fridge, "Y'all carry off Ditka."

When I came up to Ditka, he said, "No, no. You leave me alone." But I knew they were carrying Buddy off. Was he going to be the only coach up on shoulders? Oh, no. So I actually jerked Ditka up—he didn't want to go—until he was up there and finally having a good time.

It was the first time two coaches ever got carried off the field at the Super Bowl.

That was a nice moment, but the rest of the postgame celebration didn't seem like any big deal.

I remember going to the locker room and being disappointed. No champagne. There's still a Coke splash on the jersey I wore; it's in a glass frame, and everybody thinks it's blood or champagne or something. I tell 'em, "Nope, it's Coke, because the NFL didn't allow alcohol in the locker rooms."

I've always been short-changed, my whole career, in shit like that.

What was really strange, though, was that we stressed out and focused so much, and it was easy. Handed to us. It's like what most people tell you about the mountain top. It's the climb up that defines a man, not the top.

We'd gotten up there. We'd done it. What's next?

TAKING THE TROPHY HOME

You know what? I've never gotten to touch the Lombardi Trophy without a pair of gloves on.

For some reason, it never made it into my hands in the locker room or on the plane back, and it wasn't until the 15-year reunion party that I ever held it. They had the trophy there, but they had white gloves for people to put on to touch it. Something about the oil in your skin tarnishing the metal. So my skin has never caressed that trophy.

Michael McCaskey's has, though. Talk about tarnishing.

I can still see him getting off the team bus back in Chicago, holding up that trophy like "I am responsible for this."

My ass. It was George Halas, Jim Finks, Jerry Vainisi and Mike Ditka. Michael McCaskey had no input whatsoever in having that trophy in his hand.

Anyway, Chicago hadn't had a champion to celebrate in a long time, so they had a parade for us. Most of us. We set a team record with nine guys making the Pro Bowl, and all of those guys—Jimbo Covert, Richard Dent, Dave Duerson, Dan Hampton, Jay Hilgenberg, Jim McMahon, Walter Payton, Mike Singletary and Otis Wilson—went straight to Hawaii from New Orleans.

I made the AP and UPI All-Pro teams, but I definitely wasn't in Hawaii. It was about three degrees in Chicago for our parade.

There was still a multitude of people out along LaSalle Street, packed in like sardines—I guess to keep each other warm.

The street was so crowded that the people wouldn't let the buses through. The cops had to get them out of the way each foot of the way. The buses were at a crawl.

Of course, it didn't help that the windows of the buses were tinted, and people were crowding up close just to try to get a glimpse of us.

I remember this one lady, in such a fervor, jumping up on the front of the bus like she was going to try to stand on the front bumper and scream at us through the front window. She couldn't keep hold, she was slipping, and the last we saw of her was her sliding down, the bus was still moving, and her purse was still hooked onto the windshield wipers.

Like I said, nobody could see us. The fans were getting so pissed off about that, I think, they started climbing on top.

After they did that, we thought, "Why don't we get up there?" So we pulled the hatch, climbed out, and the crowd went nuts.

It gave them what they wanted—and it gave me something, too. I was cold up there, wearing just a tweed sports coat, and every other foot of the way somebody was trying to throw me a bottle of booze. Every now and then I'd catch one, drink out of it and throw it back to them.

Then we got up to the stage, and for years I got hate mail over what I said when it was my turn to talk. The only thing I said was, "That's right, Chicago, we got fucking bragging rights over the whole goddamn country now."

Because I used the Lord's name in vain, those cheap-shot Christians reared their heads again. They loved how I'd go out there and cripple another player, but don't say God's name in vain.

Chapter 8

A FAREWELL TO KINGS

STARS AND BARS

After the Super Bowl, here comes the big time. When you win, I don't care how bad or good you really are, you're a star—and you can capitalize on that name recognition.

Hell, even Mike Tomczak, the third-string quarterback on the Super Bowl team, bought a place—T'n'T's, with Tom Thayer, out in Joliet, the far west suburb of Chicago where Thayer's from. Let the good times roll. Everybody's a hero, especially the real heroes.

Walter Payton had a couple places out in Schaumburg, and it was a drive, but I'd still make it out there.

I was a regular at Ditka's City Lights. Still am at his current place downtown. And I went to all of them, from Fencik's place, the Hunt Club, to McMahon's. Even Butler had a joint.

A lot of guys got into places that didn't make it, but no matter what, most everybody made their money. Most places have a lifespan of three years anyway, then people go somewhere else because somewhere else is cooler.

Most of the deals guys had were along the lines of "Let us use your name for some of the cut." If they're just using your name, you're getting proceeds. It doesn't matter if the place goes bankrupt down the road, because you're getting checks before it does.

All I know is every time I went into one of those guys' places, they were packed—and like I said, I went in all of them. Help out the boys, you know?

Now I really believe this: To have a winning team, you've got to have some intelligent guys. And that doesn't just mean intelligent at football. You use your intelligence to be a good football player, but that intelligence works in society, too.

Ditka was always relating his team speeches to the real world. He'd talk to us like a father to his sons, laced with, "Men, you're going to find out in life..." There's a lot of aspects of life that are relatable to football—making a game plan, having a goal. That's all business. It's a natural extension to want to get into something.

NO SHOTS AT SCHOLTZ'S

Me, I fought off the entrepreneurial spirit until '89—when I bought a piece of Scholtz's Beer Garden, the oldest tavern in Texas. Eventually, every guy who gets a little money in his pocket succumbs to the dream of standing behind his own bar and pouring his buddies a free drink.

Free my ass.

I poured so many drinks on the house for me and other people that we had to take liquor out. Beer and wine only after that. Couldn't keep Crown Royal in there.

At least it was fun. Some of the boys even came down to the grand opening, too—Keith Van Horne, Tommy Thayer.

MONSTERS OF A NEW MIDWAY

After '85, Platteville became a carnival, literally. When we got big, they'd put the county fair there when we were in camp, and people from all over the area would come for a barbecue with us as the honored guests. Live bands, me and Dan would get on stage and sing with them—our staple was "Up against the Wall Redneck Mothers," and entertain the crowds.

The whole camp became the way I always envisioned George Halas's barnstorming trip with Red Grange to be. In 1925, Halas made pro football when he signed Grange for $100,000 and then took him on a coast-to-coast train ride where the Bears played 16 games in two months. It must have been a real traveling carny.

In Platteville, it wasn't like they were showing up for football any more. They were showing up for Great America. We were the Bears Theme Park.

We'd get thousands of people at every practice—more for those than for my high school football games, and that's saying something considering Texas high school football.

Everywhere, it was little kids sitting there with their big eyes looking at you.

They were there to be entertained, and I have a loud voice. All I'd have to do is say something sarcastic, and they'd roar. I was doing it for them.

There were other things, too, like when it wasn't my turn to run drills. I'd just stand over by the Gatorade bucket, and there'd be cans of the stuff sitting there. To live up to the Mongo moniker, I'd turn around toward them with a can of Gatorade and bite into the side of it with my canines, like a vampire. While it was spewing, I'd drink it down like that—oh, they'd hoot and holler.

That's when I started becoming an entertainer.

I've always been a fan of that kind of entertaiment, anyway. I like the end zone dances. Terrell Owens is a funny motherfuck-er to me. When he grabbed those pompons from a cheerleader? I fell on the floor. That's part of the experience to me.

Me being a fan of that, I wanted to give the fans some of it as well.

SPEAKING OF THE CARNIVAL

In the off season after we won the Super Bowl, I got a taste of wrestling. Jim Covert and Fridge did *Wrestlemania*, Covert because he was the Offensive Lineman of the Year and a former wrestler and Fridge because he was the Fridge. He was the biggest thing going.

I went and sat in the first row, because I was a fan.

Anyway, a Battle Royale is when all the wrestlers get in the ring and the last guy who doesn't get tossed over the top rope is the winner. They both got tossed over—but I'm pretty sure it took more than one guy to get the Fridge—and Andre the Giant won.

Those wrestling guys remembered me coming down to sit in the front row. Later, when I was in Green Bay and Lawrence Taylor was going to do another *Wrestlemania* against Bam Bam Bigelow up there, they asked me and Reggie White if we want-ed to be his All-Pro backups. Had to have the All-Pro moniker, you know.

It worked out well for me. I did the Monday show before the pay-per-view to pub the match because Lawrence was out playing golf and wouldn't do it. That led to me doing announcing one night with Vince McMahon on another one of their shows, *Raw*, and that led to me getting the announcing job on *Nitro*. I was hired to be an announcer that year after I retired, but if I wrestled I got more money.

After I wrestled and they saw how good I was at it, I just became a wrestler full time.

It was a traveling carny. You're just a sideshow dancing chicken. People paying a quarter to say, "Look at this chicken dance." They don't see the guy with the hot plate under the table turning the heat up on the chicken's feet.

But that's probably a whole 'nother book.

LOOSEN UP, GINNY BABY

The year after we won the Super Bowl, before training camp started, the Bears rented out this banquet hall for a ceremony to give all of us our championship rings. We all showed up; it was a suit-and-tie affair.

They sat Ditka with all the McCaskeys, a millworker in the middle of Martha's Vineyard. By the time the night was over, after we all got our rings, he was face-down in his plate, dead drunk.

That's the difference between the boys and the white collars the McCaskeys brought in. Heck, it might be one of the reasons the McCaskeys wanted to go white-collar.

LOOSEN UP, GINNY BABY II

The McCaskeys being the tight-ass conservatives they are, they frowned on T&A, so they fired the Honey Bears—our version of the Dallas Cowboy Cheerleaders. They told them during our Super Bowl season they wouldn't be coming back the next year. Word was they didn't think girls in short-shorts showing lots of cleavage projected a wholesome enough image for the franchise.

Of course, there were stories about the girls cavorting with the team, too. You'd get busybodies calling Halas Hall, ratting people out—allegedly.

I didn't see anything.

Wait, I didn't get married until the off season of '84, and they got rid of the Honey Bears in '85, so I suppose it's OK to say that at every level—high school, college and pro—I've always liked to have the cheerleaders around. Let me put it this way: I've dated a few at every level.

WELCOME, VINCE

Coming into '86, there wasn't a whole lot to be worried about, except for the fact that we were changing defensive coordinators, and all the talk was that the new guy, Vince Tobin, was going to change things a bunch.

Vince was the little brother of our personnel director, Bill Tobin, and hadn't coached in the NFL. He had had a couple of pretty good defenses in the USFL and Canada, and he played a style Mike Ditka liked.

Ditka always wanted to play a reading, blitz every now and then, zone defense. Let the offense make a mistake instead of Buddy's way, which was going and making the mistake happen before the offense has a chance to do something good.

Not that Ditka's way wouldn't work. There's a few philosophies out there that have won Super Bowls. It's just that I'm a fan of go get 'em.

There was some apprehension. I didn't know how this was going to work—taking attack dogs and making them sentry dogs. You don't teach an old dog new tricks, right?

But as soon as we got into the defensive meetings, Vince fixed that. He said, "We're still going to run the '46,' we're just going to call it the 'Bear defense' now."

We did some other things, too. Vince gave us the first example of a zone blitz I'd seen in the league. You're still attacking up front, but playing a zone behind it. Buddy was man-to-man, with a blitz.

Really, it was still the same attacking defensive front for us, and I loved it.

It was tough at first getting used to the terminology changes. We'd been in Buddy's system for a few years, and learning a new language wasn't easy.

Maybe it doesn't sound like much, but when the middle linebacker comes in the huddle and says, 'Bear defense,' you better not be having flashbacks or you're not going to know what that is. In the heat of battle, just that little introspective reflection of, 'OK, this used to be that and now that's this...' there's that half a step and now you're fucked.

But there's good reason for changing the terminology. The coordinator and his coaches have to be the first ones in line to know what's going on. They've got to flash quick in their minds, too. They can't be up in the booth going, "This is what we used to call it, but Buddy calls it this, so..." Too late. You've just got to get the players, through intensive meetings, to know, "This is what we're calling it now."

Most of the coverages around the league are the same anyway.

To tell you the truth, I think Vince's situation was just like when Barry Switzer inherited the Dallas Cowboys from Jimmy

Johnson. Stay out of the way. Do your best not to fuck up the machine, brother, cause it's running fine.

Vince was a genius at that. I imagine he had different ideas of what he wanted to incorporate, but if something's already working, why blow up the factory? He turned us loose, too. We got some sacks in Vince's defense.

WELCOME, AL AND TODD

Al Harris and Todd Bell came back in '86 after holding out the Super Bowl season. The way they were treated, it took their football out of them. They weren't the aggressors anymore. They were the defenders. I felt sorry for them—not for the money, but for the fact that they didn't get to go to the Super Bowl.

Of course, when they came back, we were just gonna go get another one, so they'd have theirs.

GREAT EXPECTATIONS

Heading into the season, everybody thought we were going to win another Super Bowl, me included. I didn't think there was any way we weren't going to repeat—until McMahon went down. He only played six games all year and went out for good in December after having rotator cuff surgery.

When I saw how bad the offense was struggling in practice under different signal callers, I knew we were in trouble.

I mean, you've got to recognize the signs. You know this might not work out in a game when you hear the head coach yelling constantly during offensive drills, "Run it over." You know you're in trouble.

Ed Hughes was the offensive coordinator then, but our offense was really Mike Ditka being smart enough to run Walter Payton and Jim McMahon being smart enough to know what to audible off of that. Without McMahon, no audible. It was tough. With him, we had an offense. Without him, we were just running plays.

As it would turn out, every year we went to the playoffs and we didn't have Jim McMahon starting at quarterback, I knew we'd be sucking hind tit.

The defense was enough to carry us through the regular season, but the playoffs were something different. You've got to have that stability.

I don't care if it had been Joe Montana taking his place. That offensive line trusted Jim, loved him and wanted to perform for him. It's like part of the reason I busted my ass was liking Mike Ditka and wanting him to glow about me.

Here's the best example I can give you of Jim McMahon's value. When he first got drafted, we still had training camp in Lake Forest. We had a scrimmage one day over at Lake Forest High School. It was Ditka's picked team against Buddy Ryan's picked team.

They did like a schoolyard, "I'll take him. I'll take him," and we scrimmaged.

Buddy's first pick, he didn't take Mike Singletary or Dan Hampton. He took No. 9.

WELCOME, BAMBI

Doug Flutie was supposed to solve our quarterback problems—hail the conquering hero, the Heisman winner, the guy who hadn't really been given a chance to prove himself in the NFL because he was only about five foot nothin'.

It wasn't the easiest deal for him. They brought him in late, taught him the system and threw him out there in the playoffs against the Redskins, who gave him fits.

Of course, some of his teammates did, too.

There was a lot of talk that nobody on the team liked Flutie, mostly because he had Thanksgiving dinner with Ditka, but really it was all the offensive side of the ball. I think they felt like he was the usurper to Jim McMahon's throne, so he wasn't going to be accepted.

Somebody even started calling him "Bambi," not the manliest nickname in a football locker room. I don't know who started it, but I have to admit it fit. You know, the little baby deer, how deers run around—he was kind of a prancer back there.

Me, the only problem I had with Flutie was him was throwing two fucking interceptions and fumbling the ball twice against Washington in the playoff game. I don't give a shit if he eats dinner with Ditka. If he'd have gone out there and won the Super Bowl, I'd have been fine with him being the quarterback. But he didn't.

Four fucking turnovers. We lost 27-13 to Jay Schroeder.

Of course, I don't know if Sid Luckman would have helped us against the Redskins that day. Sometimes things just don't go your way.

I mean, some days you have to beat a double-team to get free, but the quarterback holds the ball too long, so you get a sack. There was a time in this game, Schroeder's first touchdown pass, where we ran a blitz. I was on the line of scrimmage, got off with the ball, the line parted, blocking other guys, and I was set free. I ran back there as fast as I could, nobody touching me, he backed up, threw it falling over backward as I hit him. Touchdown pass. Shit happens like that, it ain't your day, baby.

FOR THE RECORD...

If I'm running the team, I'm looking around for a quarterback, too. Maybe not a midget like Flutie, but somebody.

Jim getting hurt and us having to play Flutie in the first place, that's why I love Jim, but I say it's his fault we didn't win three Super Bowls in the '80s. He was getting hurt all the time. It ain't his fault, now. But, dammit, every dynasty had one quarterback.

Ours could have been Steve Young, as I recall. Back when Tampa Bay offered him up as trade bait, Dan Hampton and I politicked to get him for the Bears, but it fell on deaf ears.

Why? Where was he from? Brigham Young. I think Jim McMahon scared them off of BYU quarterbacks.

Dan and I knew, though, from playing against Young in Tampa. We beat them, of course; they had a terrible team. But you could see the guy was good, a playmaker.

Of course, playing for us, those concussions that drove Steve out of football might have come on a little sooner—for the same reason I think it was a little bit our fault Jim was getting beat up pretty good.

Playing quarterback for the Bears, you were a marked man. Our defense hurt a lot of other teams' quarterbacks, so you know they were out to get ours.

WELCOME, BUDDY

Sometimes, I think the schedule makers just can't help themselves. They see the chance for a ratings blockbuster and they go for it, which I'm sure was one of the reasons Buddy Ryan's Eagles came to visit us in the second week of the season.

There was a lot of hype in the press, and it was a little strange having to face Buddy—but only for the defense.

I think the offense kind of enjoyed it. If I was an offensive lineman, playing against a coach I'd practiced against for years and knew what he was in the habit of calling, there'd be some things to look for, you know? Even an old shaman like Buddy had his habits. Vince sure had his. Once he got to town, if we had somebody backed up behind the 20-yard line, everybody in the huddle knew a blitz was coming.

The Eagles gave us a good game, took us to overtime before we won, and you could call that a victory for Buddy. After all, the Eagles were one of the worst teams in the league, that's why they needed a new coach in the first place, and they played the world champions to an overtime game. That's pretty good progress two games into his first year in Philly, don't you think?

To be honest, there wasn't a whole lot in the way of interaction with Buddy. I had blinders on, baby. And here's one thing about Buddy—the whole time he and I were together on the Bears, the only time he stuck around on the field after the game was when we won the Super Bowl and we carried him off the field. Buddy Ryan, after the game was over with, walked straight to the locker room every game.

You know, I didn't really shake hands much after games either. It's hypocritical to me, to get out there and go to war with somebody, not exactly being his friend if you know what I mean, and at the end shake his hand? When you've, you know, done things all afternoon? It ain't the Marquis of Queensbury out there.

TOO CLOSE FOR COMFORT

One thing we should have learned from beating the Eagles just 13-10: We were going to be in a lot of close games that year.

That's what happens when you run a read-and-react defense. When you play it safe and don't go try and make a play, the games are going to be close in the end the majority of the time. Keep the game close and in the last possession try to win it. It does work, you've got a chance, but man, why not try to make it so the game's over in the third quarter?

We went 14-2, but it wasn't an easy 14-2. Seven games were decided by six points or less and of the three times we won by more than 14, two came against Tampa Bay.

SAY WHAT?

Losing to Washington was unbelievable to me. We lost? What? I was beating shit up in the locker room afterward. Everybody was, which was a sign of how surprised we were. Most of the time, after a defeat, guys would be introspective, not showing emotion outwardly. This time, there was shouting, stuff getting hit—my locker caught hell, I know.

I think the Redskins were really up for that game as a direct result of getting their asses beat by us a couple times in the two previous years. In '84, we came in and handed them an ass-whipping in the playoffs when they were the Super Bowl champs the year before, and the way we beat them in '85, 45-10, we'd humiliated them two years in a row. That will get you up for a game, and they were ready to play.

Thing is, even with all that, nine out of 10 days, even with Doug Flutie quarterbacking, we beat them. That was their 10th day.

The one thing it didn't hurt was our confidence. We still felt we were the best team in football. We had a good year, even with the new defensive coordinator. We figured Doug Flutie wasn't going to be quarterbacking and turning the ball over six times the next time we played. What the hell, no big deal.

HULA SCHMOOLA

In '86 I made my first Pro Bowl. I went in '87, too. Didn't much like it, to tell you the truth, even with the return to the site of all my monkey bowl-grabbing glory in college, the Hula Bowl.

The Pro Bowl is scary, really. Playing on Astroturf in a game that don't mean shit, that's the time people get hurt. A freak accident, somebody falling on the side of your leg in a pickup game, more or less, might wreck your career.

We always sent a number of players to the Pro Bowl, but I wasn't a big fan of the game.

That game is almost like my Harley. I'd always wanted a Harley Davidson, but I never got one until my last year in the league, up in Green Bay—that's how much I cared about being a Packer, I guess, I got a Harley in October on my birthday when I was still playing for them. I'd never got one because you wreck, you fuck your leg up, there goes your career—how stupid is that?

BACK IN BLACK

After the playoff loss to Washington, Mike Ditka decided, "OK, we're going back to old school, we're going back to black shoes." God, how I hated those things.

Old-time religion. Black shoes. Man, those damn things made you feel sluggish, like you were slogging around in black work boots.

You know, you look in the mirror and you look sharp, you feel sharp. It gives you that bounce in your step—and that bounce is important playing football.

Dan and I tried, though. We always taped over our shoes, even though a lot of guys don't—which I think is a mistake. Put your shoe on over the tape, it's easier to roll an ankle, I think. Put tape on over your shoe, there's no way your ankle can roll as much. Anyway, once we got those black shoes, Dan and I would always have the tape cut special, so the shoes looked like Italian loafers.

POT, THIS IS KETTLE...

Ditka had one other great example of trying to keep our focus on football. He came into a morning meeting one time in '87 and—I'll never forget it—says, "You fucking guys are doing too many commercials. You need to concentrate on football."

Shit, he was doing more than anybody.

DITKA PICKS HIS SCABS

It might have taken five years, but I believe Mike Ditka laid the groundwork for getting himself fired in '87.

We went on strike that year, and they hired other players, paid them and called it NFL football. Most of the world called it scab football. During that time, Ditka lost ground with some players I don't know if he ever got back. He sided with those scab players—called them the "real Bears"—and the McCaskeys over the guys who were on strike.

There is a type of player who needs a reason to push beyond what they think is their limit—for whom? for what? Ditka ceased to be the who and the what for those guys when he sided with the scabs. Whatever part of them that played for his approval was gone.

I understood Ditka's point of view. In his mind, you sign a contract, you live up to it. We had individual contracts, but we went on strike.

The first scab game the Bears had was in Philadelphia, and it didn't draw at all—barely 4,000 people. At Soldier Field the next week, there were 32,000-plus to watch those guys.

Of course, some of them were there for us, too. We had an autograph session outside the stadium. I wasn't going to stand there holding a stick with a cardboad sign saying we were on strike.

I understood the fans who showed up were just football fans. One thing you learn after you retire is to appreciate the fans.

I was a Bear, but being a Bear wasn't mine to own. I was part of the history. The team really belongs more to the people who cheer for it than the people who play for it.

Most of the guys around the league resented the fans who showed up for those scab games. Not me. They're Bears fans. I came out to have fun with them. Here's an autograph from a real Bear, thanks for coming out.

I was there to entertain them. You know how they call some guys a players' coach? I like to think I was a fans' player.

CAN'T BLAME McMAHON

We still had a good team in '87, damn good, really. We had 70 sacks; the only guy we really lost from the year before was Gary Fencik, who retired.

But Washington caught us. They beat us in the playoffs 21-17, then went on to win the Super Bowl.

This time, it wasn't Jim McMahon's fault. He played, and the Redskins barely beat us with a punt return by that little Darrell Green, their DB, who was the fastest player in the league. We were ahead in the fourth quarter, punted the ball, and Green actually tore a cartilage in his rib cage vaulting over the top of Jim Morrissey, the last guy he got away from, scoring the winning touchdown.

We were still the local heroes, though. I wasn't hearing boos yet. Around Chicago, it was still early enough that people still remembered the Bears being not worth a shit. Here they were getting to enjoy a winning season and a playoff game, where before they never sniffed the playoffs.

I think leaving football was tough on Walter. (Photo by Daily Southtown; Tinley Park, Illinois)

FAREWELL, WALTER

The saddest thing about '87 was that it was Walter Payton's last year—not for what he did on the field, but for who he was. That's what I was sad about. Not being around him in the locker room, on the team bus, at hotels. It was like living in the same house with a brother, then he gets older and moves on with his life. He was around every now and then, but I wasn't able to enjoy him every day.

It's the nature of the business to get used to guys coming and going. But I'll always remember Walter, when we got beat by Washington that last game, sitting on the bench until the stadium was just about empty.

He sat on the end of the bench, like he was trying suck it all in and remember that little microcosm of where he was right then in his life. Just sitting there with his head down, reflecting, like the statue, *The Thinker*.

When what you're about your whole life, every waking second, is now over—man, that's a big change. That's the change large people need to make in their life to become skinnier and healthier. It's something you don't know how to do, but it's flat changing who you are.

I think that's what Walter was reflecting on: Who am I now? Who am I gonna be? And Walter had himself more together than most of the people on this planet.

WELCOME, NEAL

I have to say, the Bears really found a gem when they drafted Neal Anderson out of Florida. We were coming off the Super Bowl when we got him, so it wasn't like we had any expectation of landing a star with our low pick, but Neal was the shit.

That spark Walter had when he ran? Neal had it, too. They shared duty in '87, and Neal actually outgained Walter even though Walter got more carries.

For three years after that, Neal always gained over 1,000 yards and caught around 40 balls.

That's lightning striking twice. Neal was good. He wasn't as good as Walter, but by God he was a playmaker.

I don't think people appreciated him, though. People got spoiled with all those years of Walter. All of a sudden there's Neal carrying on. They didn't realize they'd caught lightning in a bottle twice—but there's been nothing like Neal on the Bears since.

That's what I tell people about our whole team. We spoiled you guys. Now you appreciate us, because there hasn't been anything like us since.

FAKE OR REAL?

Heading into '88, the Bears did something else I think ended up costing us.

They took the Astroturf out of Soldier Field and put natural grass in—and didn't put a heater under it. That's why in the playoffs we'd end up playing on painted green dirt. It's not like they couldn't have put a heater in, either—Green Bay'd done it, and it wasn't all that expensive, either.

Even Green Bay would turn that heater off sometimes, when a team like ours was coming to play. They'd rather have us playing on ice, so we couldn't get any forward push.

That was the mistake the Bears made with that grass field. I'm convinced it cost us winning games in the playoffs. They were thinking we were going back to the good old days, old-time football, even though we'd kicked people's asses on Astroturf.

Most people won't believe this, but I'll say it anyway. I'd have given up years off the end of my career to keep playing on Astroyurf like we'd won the Super Bowl on. I'm sure we'd have won a few more playoff games if we'd have been playing them on turf, and I'd have gladly traded the wear and tear on my body of playing on Astroturf for another shot at the Super Bowl.

In '88, it cost us playing against Montana in the NFC championship game. The field was frozen. We couldn't attack the line of scrimmage. Their offensive linemen just sat there and waited for us to come to 'em on ice skates. Our front seven, that's how we won football games, baby. We got into the backfield. You can't do that on ice. For whatever reason, on Astroturf, you wouldn't get that ice on top—even though it was hard as ice underneath.

PAGING DR. HAMPTON, DR. McMICHAEL

On November 2, 1988, Mike Ditka had a heart attack.

I'm tempted to say "allegedly," because the way he came back, you could almost think it was a ruse to get the team fired up. Vince Tobin assumed the couching reins, but not two weeks after it happened, Mike was standing there on the sideline in Washington, just watching—with his heart specialist making sure he was not going to go overboard, I guess.

He took over from Tobin the next week in Tampa.

It was like he had no convalescence. But then, based on what happened the day he fell ill, he might have figured he needed to get back quick.

The day it happened, it was big news, and we were watching on the monitors in the locker room. The cardiologist came on and said, "No more drinking and smoking." That was our cue, baby.

Up in his office, it was more of a cigar bar than a coach's office. Ditka had nice Cubans, whatever you wanted, in humidors up there. He had nice sipping whiskey and brandy and stuff like that. Dan and I went up there and barged into his office while he was lying in the hospital bed, stealing his cigars and his bottles. But we didn't steal them for ourselves; we went and handed them out to the team.

It was all out of concern for the coach, pure and simple.

FOGETABOUTIT

I've seen some crazy shit in my time, but one of the craziest was something just about everybody else couldn't see, no matter how hard they tried. Too bad, too, because it was our first playoff win in three years—against Buddy Ryan, to boot.

In '88, Buddy started spouting off about how great his defense was—better than his Bears defense, he was telling folks. Now any defense with Reggie White rushing the passer was going to be good—but they weren't monsters like us.

So here come the playoffs, on New Year's Eve no less, and here come Buddy's Eagles.

Then the lights went out. I think it was God's way of putting a pall over the whole thing.

You could tell it was going to be a weird day. The weather was real funky, but when this fog came in off Lake Michigan just before halftime, it was like nothing I'd seen. It just started settling down, lower and lower, until the people in the stands

We beat Buddy in the fog bowl, but that pox Montana finished our season a week later. (Photo by **Daily Southtown; Tinley Park, Illinois)**

couldn't see a damn bit of what was going on on the field. On TV, it was like watching no channel—snow. Unbelievable.

From my point of view, though, it looked worse than it was. On field level, you could see the guys on the other sideline. Fog, you know, it's a little off the ground.

But a long pass? Forget about it.

Randall Cunningham had one picked off by Maurice Douglass, but I never saw it. I just heard the fans cheering, and I still don't know how they saw it.

However it happened, we beat them, then played San Francisco in the conference championship.

You can thank the frozen grass for us losing 28-3. It would have been a different story on Astroturf or even with a heater under the grass where we could sink our cleats in and try to get Joe. Years later, when I was with Green Bay, one of the Packers coaches who was with San Francisco at the time told me Montana was so cold he couldn't feel his hands, and he still beat us.

Damn pox.

TEXTBOOK TACKLES

There is one thing from '88 I'm pretty proud of. When Dan Hampton was being inducted years later into the Hall of Fame, he said, "There was a point in time when my friend Ming and I played the best ever."

That was in '88. Dan played defensive tackle that year, and there were no two defensive tackles playing side by side who ever played better in tandem than we did that year.

It was the only year I ever led the team in sacks, with 11 1/2, and Dan got nine and a half. We both had 88 tackles, tied for third on the team behind Singletary and Duerson.

That year, they were double-teaming both of us. The center and one guard would turn on one of us, and they'd leave the fullback in to help the other guard with the other one. You don't ever see that—the fullback just stepping up to help the guard every time. It was unbelievable.

We had one better year sacks-wise, in '84, when he had 11 1/2 and I had 10. That's when he was playing defensive tackle again. When we played tackle together, we fucked shit up.

Dan never really liked playing tackle before that. I had to talk him into moving from end in '84. When they suggested it, he rebelled. I convinced him that, out on the end, you only make the play when it comes to your side of the field. At tackle, you're like the middle linebcker; both sides of the field are open for you to make plays.

Even after '85, when they brought Fridge in and moved Dan back to end in the base defense, he was inside in the 46 defense—which, of course, we played a lot.

Most of the time, the 46 would look like this: Otis and Wilber would be on the same side, the left, either both outside the tackle or one of them on the tight end and the other outside of that. I'd be in the gap between the tackle and the guard. Dan was over center. William would be in the other guard/tackle gap and Richard would be on the outside, like Otis and Wilber, usually on the weak side, while Mike Singletary would be stacked up right behind Dan.

The strong safety would always make a lot of plays in that defense, because he'd be more or less a baby linebacker on the strong side. There was always an open area between Mike and the linebackers on the line, or between Mike and Richard, that the strong safety would step in and fill. The strong safety would make plays because the running back, on his cutback, usually perceived that area to be open.

Whatever. All I knew was, when Dan was at tackle, it was like I was free. Because he was so good, they had to worry about him, it set me free to do some things I wanted to do.

There were times when the center had to turn to him. I knew that gap was going to be open for me to come inside that guard and get up in the quarterback's face.

There were games in the 46 that were almost like magic. They couldn't stop us. Dan would hit to my side and hold the center; then I'd loop around. The tackle would always try to block down on me in the 46, to make sure I wasn't going to try to come around outside. So I'd go at the tackle like I was going outside of him, then the guard would think he's free to pick up Dan.

All Dan had to do was grab the center and hold him; I'd fake outside the tackle and come around Dan free while he shielded three guys.

The difference with Fridge was his sheer presence, taking up that much space, I knew the ball wasn't going to go there. The run, the quarterback stepping up in the pocket, or having an open field of vision, none of that was going to happen through Fridge.

LAST MAN STANDING

Look, you get used to people leaving in football. Happens every year. I mean, Fencik retired after the '86 season, Walter after '87. Otis Wilson tore up his knee in '87 playing defensive end in the nickel package on a muddy field in Green Bay—he came back after that and played for the Raiders, but it wasn't the same old Otis. Wilber Marshall and Willie Gault were on other teams starting in '88.

But '89? Worst year of my football life.

McMahon was gone, to San Diego, and with him went our offensive heart. We went from moving men on a chess board to running plays. But that was just the start.

Even so, the year started out great. Dan played in the first four games, we went 4-0; then he hurt his knee.

Dan missed the rest of the season, and we won two more games.

At one point, we were 6-4, Ditka said, "We might not win another game," and we didn't. I don't know why he said it, but by God it was prophetic.

As the injuries mounted, our season began to unravel. (Photo by Daily Southtown; *Tinley Park, Illinois)*

There were reasons. William broke his arm. Richard broke something in his leg and was gone. Dan hurt his knee and was gone. Hell, Singletary and I were the only two guys on the defense to start all 16 games. We were the last men standing. I was looking around the huddle not recognizing anybody.

Like I said, worst year of my football life. Capped by a 26-0 loss at San Francisco to finish 6-10.

Chapter 9

RANDOM NOTES FROM TRAIL'S END

MAKING CONCESSIONS, RATINGS

When Dave Duerson went to the Giants for the '90 season, I took his TV gig. In the old days, that would've been impossible—football blinders on, got no time to do something so frivolous.

It was me making concessions. My football career was on the down side. Here's another avenue. I could be an entertainer.

I should probably still be getting a cut of Mark Giangreco's paycheck. Eventually, he became the highest-paid local TV sports guy in town, but when I joined his Sunday night show—everybody did extra sports on Sundays during football season when we were big—he was more or less low man on the totem pole going up against guys at the other stations who'd been around longer—Tim Wiegel and Johnny Morris, who was an ex-Bear and had Mike Ditka on his Sunday show.

The way Giangreco was trying to gain his notoriety was by being the negative, sarcastic fuck of the media. Ditka hated him. Probably still does.

One of the reasons I took that job was the heel always needs to get his. Before it was ever seen on TV, I'd already seen in my mind these flashes of brilliance, these pearls I was going to cast before swine, of the things I was going to do to him live on camera.

Weekly, I'd do something slapstick to him, and the people loved it. I imagine Ditka was getting a chuckle out of it himself, even though he was doing his show over on Channel 2. In fact, Ditka's show won a local Emmy one year, but once Giangreco added me, we'd beat him in the ratings as often as not.

My personal favorite thing I ever did to Giangreco was one that went along with the old expression about having egg on your face when you've talked out of turn.

In '90, he picked us to go 8-8. Well, we won the division, and we're in the playoffs, and the night we won the division, I took a raw egg into the studio and slapped it on his forehead. I said, "Don't you have egg on your face now?"

There were others, though.

I used a chainsaw on him—a fake one given to me by this comic, the Amazing Jonathon. He was a fan of the show and had all kinds of gimics, and he sent me a fake chain saw that, when you pressed a button, squirted fake blood all over the place. So I fired that thing up and it looked like I was cutting him up, cutting him up.

There was whipped cream, the spitting snake, cutting his tie off, holding him down while my wife at the time put makeup on him. What didn't I do to that poor man?

I'd wait for the inevitable sarcastic, negative comment, then I'd blast him.

Giangreco was OK with it, because he knew it was working for ratings, and he knew I was making a joke out of myself. The heat was on me. He had a line with the station that I wasn't going to shit on. The integrity of him reading off the teleprompter, that was off limits.

Besides, there was always a method to my madness. I knew there was a cliff, a line I could go over and fall straight down. The juggling act is to get right there and make people think you were fixing to fall off, then not. The time the little red light was on me, that's when they got the juggling act. He didn't know it was coming, but he more or less trusted me.

Station management wasn't always so sure, right from the start.

The first show, I'd had a pretty good game in the opener, we beat Seattle, so before the red light came on I said, "Mark, ask me how I'm doing."

He did, and I launched into, "Well, Mark, when I went to take my constitutional after the game, I didn't know if it was hemorrhoids dripping blood in the water or the wife's Lee Press-On Nail finally dissolved."

I heard the producers yell from the booth, and those are sound-proof. The first break, there's the phone ringing off the hook under the desk.

What did I say that hadn't been said on TV? You get commercials for hemorrhoids and Lee Press-On Nails both.

I ended up getting fired, as I recall, for something along the lines of, "This is what I think you meant by saying that."

Of course, I did get accused by Jenny Jones, the talk-show hostess, of spray-painting a mustache and a goatee on her big picture in the lobby. All I can say is boys will be boys after a football game and one too many toddies. Might have been Kevin Butler along with me, instigating.

I did happen to have spray paint along with me to use on the show.

To tell you the truth, I was kind of glad it was over. It had become a weekly thing; what was I going to do next? It was almost a distraction from football.

In the end, that show was sort of like Marilyn Monroe. It died an early death and left a pretty corpse.

AGING WELL

When you get away from it after a time, the things you most remember, the things you're most proud of, are the things you did in the game as an old man. You've really got to be knowledgeable, you've really got to be on top of it, to make the plays as an old man that you did as a young man.

I had that talk with Reggie White, when we did a wrestling show when I was with the Packers. He was getting ready to quit, but he came back, played a couple more years and did some great things. He wasn't the Reggie White of old, but I guarantee you he enjoyed every minute of it.

Actually, I told the same thing to Jerry Rice. My wife, Misty, was with me when I was wrestling, doing a card show in Dallas. They had football players too, and Jerry Rice was there right after he'd hurt his knee. He knew from years of scouting reports I'd had my knee problems, so I was a guy he could talk to about it. Backstage he came up and said, "I've probably lost a step now. Should I retire?" I said, "Jerry, when you've got two steps on everybody, you can afford to lose one."

He's still playing and scoring touchdowns. I guarantee you he's prouder of himself for what he's doing now than if he'd retired after he'd thought he lost a step.

PRESIDENT WILLIAM, SERGEANT MING

Women sometimes say men only grow older, they don't grow up, and I guess you might could prove it by some football players.

William Perry and I, for example, had a clubhouse sitting beside Halas Hall. It was a groundskeeper's shed, but it was like our little kid's fort. William was the president, I was the sergeant at arms, and if somebody didn't belong in there it was, "Get out." Think of Spanky and Our Gang, "No Girls Allowed," but with the "s" backwards, that was about our mentality.

After practice we'd go in there—me and William and whoever we deemed worthy. We'd tell the old stories, have our little bottles of booze hidden around, have a couple drinks. We'd end up making the equipment guys wait late, because we'd still have to take our showers and change after our meetings.

William was the president because he was like the groundskeeper's assistant, like Bill Murray's character, Carl, in *Caddyshack*. William seriously liked to cut grass. Every once in a while he'd just have to tend to the grounds, so he'd head for the shed.

One time, there was no key to be had and William wanted to cut some grass. There's the riding lawnmower, and I said, "Now, Goddammit, William, don't mess up that lawnmower. Wait for him to come tell you where the key is."

He said, "Don't worry about it, I'm a MacGyver," like the TV show where the guy could build a bomb out of a paper clip. He started that mother up—hot-wired a lawnmower.

STARTS AND FINISHES

Dan Hampton had gotten hurt in '89, I want to say his 12th knee operation as a result. We all knew right away he was coming back for his last hurrah in '90.

I came into that season with 101 straight starts, but it was a little crowded on the D-line that year with me, Dan and William at tackles, plus Richard Dent and Trace Armstrong, coming off a decent rookie season, at the ends. My starting streak got screwed up because we went with a three-man rotation at tackle, which meant half the games I didn't start.

So my starting streak got messed up, but I still ended up setting Bears records for most games and most consecutive games played, both 191.

It says in my bio in old Bears media guides my start streak ended in the first game in '90 because I missed training camp with a contract dispute, but it was really about the rotation. They can say what they want.

Dan and William had been the ones in camp doing the work; they deserved to start in the rotation that first day, in my mind.

MONEY MATTERS

When I held out—and I did twice, in '89 and '90—I always used to catch hell in the press about "the sanctity of the contract." My ass. Where the hell is the sanctity now that there's a salary cap, and instead of honoring the contract management says, "We'll cut you and bring you back for less money?"

There's no sanctity there. Fucking hypocrites.

At one point, the Bears had enough and decided to threaten me with a trade. The Houston Oilers were willing to trade for me, and that didn't sound too bad to an old Texas boy; then all of a sudden the Bears came up with some money.

To that point, I believe Larry Csonka and I were the only two guys in NFL history to hold out, with a contract, two years in a row.

They doubled my salary after I went to the Pro Bowl in '86 and '87. I was making $500,000, but there were still guys making a million while I was making all the plays. I didn't care what contract I signed. I wanted them to show appreciation to me the only way ownership can show a player appreciation—with money.

Ditka was even kind of on my side. I knew how he felt about contracts and holdouts, but he told the press something like, "In this case, I think Steve McMichael deserves it."

I did a lot of the negotiating myself, not always with the most pleasant circumstances, but I think it was the right way to go. Most players find out agents are the biggest scam since two-man beach volleyball got put on television.

All an agent does is go to the owner and say, "How much you giving him?" Then he goes to the player and says, "This is the offer, do you want to take it?" Player says no, agent goes back, "He said no."

He's just a go-between. You can do that yourself.

Even so, when I started out, I had an agent—the same guy as Dan. When I became an All-Pro, having the same agent as another All-Pro defensive lineman on the same team wasn't a good thing. I dropped him. My friend Larry Bales and I went into partnership in a bar in Texas. He was a lawyer and a politician, and he wanted to take a stab at being an agent. So I let him come along in these negotiations.

He'd meet with Ted Phillips, the Bears' money man in those days before he replaced Michael McCaskey as president and CEO, when I wasn't around. When I'd come back, things would get said.

Ted still talks about it to this day, and I swear I don't remember it, but he says when the negotiations ended on the last contract I signed, I got up, leaned over the desk and said, "I'd like to hit you right in the fucking mouth."

A lot of people might have liked to do it, but I'll take Ted's word for it that I was the one who actually said it.

A FINE USE OF FINES

One of the times I held out, the Bears extended my contract and bumped it up a little. They gave me a signing bonus, which made up the difference of the fines I was accruing not being in training camp.

One of the favorite things I ever did in football was with that money from the fines. I got to select which charity it'd go to, and it was $70,000 or $80,000.

Part of it went to refurbish the terminal children's ward at a hospital on the West Side of Chicago. They got new TVs, carpeting, games for the kids and things. Another part went to our team preacher's church. Father Nick's church had a little kindergarten on the side of the church, and a tornado wiped it out. They got the money and rebuilt the kindergarten.

It wasn't about the money. There wasn't a press conference. I had a chance to give, so I did. I think most players in the league are like that. Most guys don't need a celebrity golf tournament with their name on it. Most of the guys I knew in football were good guys who wanted to do good things.

DAN'S LAST STAND

It became apparent pretty early in Hampton's last game that it was gonna be Hampton's last game. We were playing the Giants in the playoffs, the year Jeff Hostetler took them to the Super Bowl. Sometime in the first couple of series, I actually got back there, sacked him, and caused a fumble that Trace Armstrong recovered. But I knew we were going to get beat that day when the offense ended up getting down to their goal line, went for it four straight plays and didn't get in. I knew our offense wouldn't do shit against their defense that day.

Comes down to the end of the game and the Giants, for whatever reason, were trying to rub it in. They already had the game in a blowout, but it was 24-3, last minute of the game, and they were still trying to score a touchdown.

We were in a huddle in our own end zone. Dan was usually quiet in the huddle, but this time, before Singletary can call out the defense, Dan stood up and said, "Guys, don't let 'em score on the last play of my career."

Touchdown.

I apologized to him afterward in the locker room on behalf of all the guys.

HOT NUTS, ANYONE?

We all know football is an emotional game, and anyone can tell you sometimes emotions blur—laughing at a funeral, crying at a wedding, that kind of thing.

Similar things can happen when attempts at inspiration take a wrong turn into comedy. It could really happen to Mike Singletary, who was never funny unless it was on accident, and the accident usually happened when he was trying to be his most serious.

Knowing he wasn't trying to be funny about it made the stuff that came out of his mouth the funniest things you could hear somebody say.

One year, the year after that second Redskins loss in the first round of the playoffs, we're getting ready for our first playoff game. Mike's up there and he's just lost it. He's fixing to lead calisthenics, but that's the time the spirit moves him to give a team speech.

The guy considers himself a minister—and I've got to give him his props for his convictions, he means it when he's carrying his Bible around—but he's really lost it this time. Expletives are flowing out of his mouth, he's preaching up a storm, screaming, "I refuse to go home early. Get your goddamn nuts hot!"

I fell out laughing. Get your nuts hot? I still give him hell about that. I think it means get fired up and have some balls, but he just put them together.

PULL UP A CHAIR, KID

Mark Carrier, a safety out of USC, was a rookie in '90, and he was in awe of me and Hampton. Strangest thing was, the first thing we noticed is how bad his hands were.

It's strange because when Mark was a rookie he set the team record with 10 interceptions in a season.

But it's like Fencik found out—with our pass rush, most of the passes that came down the middle were floating passes that most of the time you could catch like a punt. We'd come in, the quarterback would throw off his back foot and throw up a floater. Brett Favre was the only guy who could throw it off his back foot and still zing that thing in there like he was stepping through it.

That year, Mark saw a lot of floaters he could close in on.

He saw a lot of things, sitting around our team breakfasts like a groupie. The day of the game, we'd do a lot of what I'm doing right now, sitting around the table telling stories, and Mark Carrier would be sitting around wide-eyed, taking it all in.

Actually, it was nice to see. Not all of the guys the McCaskey regime brought to the team, but more than I'd care to recall, were more business than football. It was their job, not their love.

I didn't have a lot in common with those guys.

That's why I appreciated the Mark Carriers.

Anybody you saw on the field busting their ass, doing whatever they could to win that one game that day—not saving themselves for the year, not waiting to turn it on in the playoffs—those are the guys I appreciated.

THE ARMSTRONG OF THE LAW

Trace Armstrong was one guy who knew it was a business—hell, we called him the clubhouse lawyer, and he eventually became the president of the players' union—but he could separate himself from that on game day.

Trace was studying to be a lawyer, so talking to him in the locker room was to talk about the law, the judicial world, the courtrooms of America. But on the field, he was different, a pure player—after a fashion.

At first, he was gangly, clumsy even. He was like a marionette, how they dangle and flop around—that's what he looked like in practice to me when he first got up here after we drafted him out of Florida in '89.

Dan and I looked at each other like, "Oh, no."

But even the most intelligent guys in the world like me can be wrong.

Now, though, I'm proud of his career. I helped teach him football, him playing left end right next to me.

REFRIGERATED FEAR

Donnell Woolford was quite a little striker when he first came to us as a cornerback out of Clemson in '89. But one day he found out firsthand how heavy William Perry was when he fell

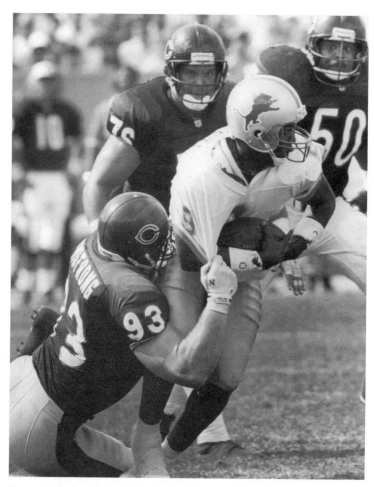

It was my pleasure to help Trace Armstrong become an outstanding player. (Photo by **Daily Southtown;** *Tinley Park, Illinois)*

on you. I have to say, it kind of crushed the physical right out of Donnell.

Donnell came up to force the play on a quick throw in the flat. William Perry broke out that way and got there just in time to pile on without getting a flag. Donnell was underneath, and

William just about squished the life out of him. It actually hurt him somewhere, and Donnell was never quite so physical after that.

THIS ONE'S FOR YOU, COACH

During the '91 season, Mike Ditka won his 100th game in his 10th season as our coach. After the game, in the locker room, I stood up and gave him the game ball.

He had always been the one in the locker room handing out the game balls. He gave me a few, for sure—I think I've got 30. But that was a milestone that needed to be recognized.

I got up and said to everybody, "Think about that. One hundred wins in 10 years—that'll get you in the playoffs every year, won't it?"

Somebody needed to say something about him and I did. He played it down. Didn't want to show anything. Didn't have to, I knew how he felt—even if I only heard it once.

The year he got fired, '93, I walked in the locker room after a loss and the guys were kind of nonchalant. To me, you show the loss some respect by being somber, not laughing. I walk in, there's some guys over on one side laughing, guys over in another corner saying, "Where we going tonight?" Another guy's standing with the press, talking to everybody about what he did.

My locker was all the way across the room from where I was standing. I took my helmet, threw a strike into it. Boom! the noise reverberated through the room. For the rest of the time I was in that room, it was somber, and in the quiet I heard Ditka from the coach's office say, "I love that guy."

I feel the same way. I don't just like Mike Ditka, I love him—he was the coach I was supposed to play for, you know?

McCASKEY FAMILY PLANNING

I'll say this for Michael McCaskey's tenure as president of the Bears: I promise you, during that time the Bears made money, and what else would a businessman want to put on his resume?

As far as the business part of the Bears goes, he did a hell of a job. But when it came to knowing football, knowing the mentality and what makes up all the different facets of a football team, Mike came up a little short. You need pawns and knights and castles on a chess board, not all pawns; everyone has to have different talents, and I think Michael McCaskey was in love with scouting combine types. Run fast, jump high, score well on the psychological tests, you're his guy.

But here's some scouting wisdom: I don't care how fast or how high you jump. If you didn't make a play in college, you damn sure aren't gonna make one in the pros.

There's got to be heart to go along with God's physical gifts.

I don't know why Michael underestimated heart, because there was plenty of it in his family. His grandfather, George Halas, had it. His mother and George's daughter, Virginia McCaskey, had it—and I'm sure Virginia, in her time being around the team in the earliest Monsters of the Midway days—saw something besides these Marquis of Queensbury, white-collar guys Michael favored.

God bless Virginia's husband, Ed McCaskey, who was the team's chairman of the board from the time George Halas died until 1999, then was chairman emeritus until he died in 2003. I liked that old man. He knew what was going on. He'd come through the locker room, basically the owner of the team as Virginia's husband, but he was a players' owner.

He'd talk to the guys, come into the training room with me and Dan and say something like, "OK, I'm going to the track today, I've got a winner. You guys want in on it?" Stuff like that.

That stuff was always out of Mike's realm. He's not personable like that. He's dry.

THE DEATH OF DITKA

Seems to me Mike Ditka should have gotten more rope than the McCaskeys gave him at the end. Sure, we went 5-11 in '92, but we'd been in the playoffs seven of the previous eight years.

I believe Ditka wanted more control over who was being brought to the team, and by this time he was getting less. Jerry Vainisi, his good friend and the Bears' general manager after Jim Finks resigned in '83, was replaced in '87 by Bill Tobin—a McCaskey guy.

I promise you, Michael couldn't wait for an excuse to get rid of Mike Ditka so the team would be his.

In '92, Ditka finally gave him that excuse—the tantrum that just about broke Jim Harbaugh.

We were in Minnesota, winning 20-0 in the fourth quarter. Ditka called a run and Harbaugh audibled to a flat pass. He threw an interception for a touchdown, and we went on to lose the game 21-20.

Jimmy wasn't a bad quarterback. It took some time for him to adjust to the pros after getting drafted out of Michigan in '87, but he had some pretty good years for us and went to the Pro Bowl later with Indianapolis. He just called the wrong audible that day.

This is why Ditka went off on Jim: When you're up 20-0 in the fourth quarter, you run the damn ball. You don't audible to a pass. I promise you, Ditka had gone over that in meetings.

Harbaugh audibled to a pass, it got picked off and run back for a touchdown, Ditka went off.

I don't think Harbaugh completed another pass that day. I'm sure, after the Vikings went up 21-20, that Ditka wanted him to.

If you look at it from the McCaskeys' point of view, it's like, "He cut my quarterback's nuts off and he didn't complete a pass after that."

That was the death of Ditka, basically, the last time he lost a Bears player after he started losing them during the '87 strike.

TRUE CONFESSION

To tell you the truth, the stage my career was at when Ditka left was almost becoming drudgery. The sheer repetition of every day—Monday come in and watch the previous game, Tuesday you're off, Wednesday you do what you've always done on Wednesday for years. Now Dave Wannstedt comes in with new terminology, new philosophy, it rejuvenated me in a way. It was a new challenge.

Setting goals is a big thing to do in life. It's the climb up the mountain that defines the man, not the time at the top. Hell, you get to the top and what do you see? Other mountains—and you say to yourself, "I want to climb that one."

WANNY'S WORLD

Dave Wannstedt was the hot candidate, and Michael McCaskey went and got him. Dave was the defensive coordinator for the Cowboys, who had just won the Super Bowl, and their defense was a big reason they started their decade of dominance in the '90s.

The fact that they got that decade started against us with a playoff win in '91 probably didn't hurt Dave's chances any.

Dave's scheme was about putting guys in the gap and getting up the field. At first I thought, "Great, this puts me in automatic pass rush mode. I don't have to read offensive linemen anymore. I just get in a gap and go."

What it did was get my ass double-teamed. Offensive linemen are going to squeeze you, make sure you don't get through the gap, then they've got time to go get somebody else.

I'd sort of get away from the system, though, by doing what we called holding the jump-through for the linebacker.

It was something Dan and I had done constantly in the old days.

Mike Singletary had a habit of coming up to me before every game and posing me a question: "Who's the best middle linebacker in the game, Steve?"

He'd expect the response, "You are, Mike, go show 'em today."

Then he'd say, "Take care of me today." That meant hold the offensive linemen so they couldn't get off on him.

All I had to do was grab the guys double-teaming me and Singletary's running free.

Wannstedt was about getting up the field, don't hold anybody, because the linebacker's job is to get in his gap. His idea was get in that gap, and when somebody gets off you, you make the play. I kept holding the jump-through, and look at how many tackles Dante Jones had that year—189.

We were 7-9, and I figure we lost nine games where the other team was running the ball. A middle linebacker makes more tackles in a losing season than a winning one, because teams are running at you, winning the game.

RIDDLE ME THIS

I liked Dave. I didn't like what he and just about every other defensive coordinator to ever get promoted to head coach did.

What's the thing he did to get the job? Coach defense.

Why not hire an offensive coordinator to run the offense and stay on the headset running the defense? Why do they all start thinking, "This is what I want to run on offense," when that's not their expertise?

Bob Slowik was his defensive coordinator, and he just left it up to Bob. I'm sure he and Dave went over it during the week, but in the final analysis it was Bob on the sideline calling the defensive plays. It should've been Dave doing that.

BACK TO YOU, JOHN

We played three Thanksgiving Day games during my time with the Bears and didn't win one until the last of them—but that's the one you might say left a bad taste in my mouth.

We were playing the Lions; John Madden's crew was there, so that meant he was going to make a big to-do of giving a turkey leg to the game's MVP.

We held Barry Sanders to basically nothing and won 10-6, so John decided he was going to give his turkey legs to the four defensive linemen—me, Trace Armstrong, Chris Zorich and Richard Dent.

We were already in the locker room, and they had to call us back out onto the field for them to talk to us after the game. They had only two headsets, and Madden told them, "Give the headsets to Dent and Zorich." That hurt. So I was just standing there eating a turkey leg while he was trying to talk to those two.

John's humor—Chris Zorich and Richard Dent were just not getting it. Finally, they were standing there mute long enough and Madden said, "Well, give the headset to McMichael."

Naturally, I've got to retort, "John, these turkey legs are as dry as your humor." And I flung it away.

John's had a problem with me ever since.

But then, I've had a problem with him longer. In '85, he picked the whole defense to make his All-Madden team—I've still got the poster—but every year after that I never made it. I always figured I was a blue-collar guy, down in the trenches, a tough guy who kind of seemed like an All-Madden annual pick. And he never took me.

Sharing the Madden Thanksgiving Turkey with my teammates. Coach Madden didn't appreciate my "dry" humor.

WEARING THE GREEN AND GOLD

God forgive me, but I ended my career as a Green Bay Packer. Hey, I began it as a Patriot, and don't tell me I wouldn't have heard that a little more often if the Super Bowl had gone the other way.

But I want to tell every fan in Chicago that when I went to Green Bay in '94, the Bears had fired me. They said, "We're not giving you any more money." The Packers called up and said, "We'll give you a half million dollars." Is anybody in the habit of giving back a winning lottery ticket? I don't think so.

After '93, Dave Wannstedt gave me two choices. He said, "Steve, salary cap reasons, if you come back, we'll bring you back for $300,000." I was scheduled to make $1 million that year. He said, "You'll be in the rotation, but you won't be starting."

Then he said, "Or you can come be my defensive line coach."

I said, "Coach, I still got the fever, I still want to play ball, so I'm going to see if somebody else wants to hire me."

The Bears found out the Packers were offering some money; they just said, "Let him walk."

It wasn't bad, outside of playing the Bears twice. I still got to play the whole NFL. We made the playoffs—Dallas beat us, but it was still a good year.

Green Bay really only got half of me. I tore a knee ligament off in training camp, so I was playing on first down, didn't hardly ever get to pass rush.

Call it karma, or kismet, or whatever, but old immediate Steve made a concession, and it cost him. I wanted to show Brett Favre and his teammates I was one of the boys, so I brother-in-lawed it in a practice. Never did it in Chicago. Do it one time in Green Bay and I tore ligament in my knee, right off the bone.

In a drill, I beat the guard, and he was off balance after I ran by him. He was scrambling, down low, trying to keep up with me, and right in front of me was Favre.

Most of the time in Chicago, I'd run by and just slap the shit out of the quarterback, let him know I'm there. This time, I started shutting it down to slow down in front of Brett. He saw me coming and started to reverse pivot like he was going to spin and run outside. He was going slow, making a joke out of getting away from me, and I saw that, so I stopped, and I was going to turn the other way, because I knew on the film it was going to look like we were dancing. But when I stopped, that guard caught up with me, pinned me back over my leg, and I heard that ligament snap.

Even so, I told the head coach, Mike Holmgren and the defensive coordinator, Fritz Shurmur, "Hey, I'm probably gonna lose a step, but this is my last hoo-rah, so I ain't gonna get it operated on. My legs are strong enough to make the season." They're like, "What?" So I took them down to the weight room, put 725 pounds on the bar and did three reps squatting with that bad ligament. Holmgren said, "Well, I guess you can do it." I played the year, my last one.

I was still being hard-headed, thinking I could still play, until Barry Sanders went the distance on me in Detroit. A play I'd always made just wasn't there.

Granted, Barry was a guy I could miss three times on one play when I was healthy. He could back up faster than I could chase him.

He cut inside, then cut back into the gap where the defensive end should've been, but wasn't. The play I'd always made, to come back out and make the tackle, the knee wasn't there, it gave. He was gone. That's when I knew it was over.

SOLDIERING ON

The most enduring memories of that last year, naturally, came from Soldier Field. At one point, the Bears ran a fourth and one play right at me and I stuffed it. I never felt more guilty.

I shouldn't have. We—the Packers, I mean—ended up winning 33-6.

The cosmos was crying, baby. That was the Monday night they finally retired Dick Butkus's jersey. I came back to Soldier Field as a Packer, and it was like a hurricane. A monsoon. Water was just standing on the field, coming down too quick to run off.

It was like the heavens unbound. Add in the throwback jerseys we were wearing—the Bears had these striped deals, just about the ugliest things I'd ever seen—and it was like a timeless game, one for the ages.

And I was a Packer. God forgive me.

PACKER WHACKERS

All this talk about my time in Green Bay makes me think back to how much I hated those bastards at one point.

In the Ditka-Forrest Gregg heyday, I'd heard through the grapevine that Gregg told his players something along the lines of, "I don't care if it's illegal. Take them out."

That's when the rumors started hitting that we had had personal bounties out on guys. But I'm not going to confirm or deny it.

If anybody wants to pay heed to it, fine. But I'm not confirming or denying.

A sight that probably still burns the eyes of most Bears fans.

I will say, never put a bounty on a guy who's wearing your same number on the other team. There was a Packer named Brian Noble who went down in a game and he wore No. 99.

I'm not confirming or denying, but there could have been a guy named Dan Hampton standing up in a meeting going,

"Brian Noble, fuck him, bounty on him." I believe the records will show Dan went down in that game, too.

Let's just say there was a possibility Dan went down that game.

I'm telling you, when the commissioner heard about this, there was an investigation into criminal charges.

It was seriously ugly back then. That was the year Kenny Stills hit Matt Suhey about a year after the whistle and some nobody named Mark Lee took Walter Payton way out of bounds over the Bears' bench—though, really, Walter knew he was going, and he was so strong he held onto Lee and took him with him.

Then there was '86, when Charles Martin had his "hit list" towel, with a bunch of Bears names on it. Martin body-slammed Jim McMahon on his shoulder and right out of the lineup, and guess whose name was on the top of Martin's list?

Part of me takes that as a show of respect, like, "We can't beat you guys legal, so we've got to do it dirty."

On the other hand, body-slamming McMahon did lead to Flutie in the playoffs that year...

Chapter 10

MONGOISMS AND OTHER FLOTSAM

MONGOISM #1

A coach isn't somebody who just tells you where to go in a defensive scheme. He shows you how to get there.

STRONG MEN

If I hadn't been as strong as I was, I wouldn't have gotten near as far as I did.

I had a reputation for bending bars in the weight room, but there were some others.

Jimbo Covert, doing squat reps at like 800 pounds, had the strongest legs of anybody before he hurt his back. The Fridge never put the time in weight room because he was so naturally

Tom Thayer was one of the stronger guys on the team. (Photo by Daily Southtown; Tinley Park, Illinois)

strong, but the things I had to work my ass off to get to, he'd come in there and just do naturally.

Tommy Thayer was plenty strong. I saw him in Atlanta, where we were training the week before we went to the Super Bowl, bench-press over 500 pounds. During the season, that's pretty damn strong. In the off season, I'd be benching over 500 on occasion, but as the season wears on, damn...

Really, we had four or five guys on the team who would bend bars, literally. I was always doing it because I benched with a close grip. You don't go out on the football field and do a nice, slow press with an offensive lineman; it's as quick as you can do it.

So I used to pound reps out with that close grip. Quick-twitch muscles are what football is all about. Doing that with 500 pounds on the bar tended to leave a few of them bent.

A FINAL THOUGHT ON THE POX

Joe Montana, for all his mobility, might have ended up being one of the easiest quarterbacks in the league to sack. Fat lot of good it did.

After playing Joe for a couple of years, he knew we were coming and we were trying to hurt him, to hit him hard. He'd see you coming and he'd just fall down. Now it's second and 17, he stands up and throws a pass to Jerry Rice for 20 yards, and that sack didn't mean shit—and he didn't have to take any punishment for it, because of the way he'd gone down.

Outfoxed by the pox.

MONGOISM #2

I'd always had a love-hate relationship with the fans in Chicago. You get enough of walking in at halftime getting booed. And I'm not talking because we were losing; I'm talking because we weren't covering the spread.

ATTENTION TO DETAIL

OK, I might have had a slight problem with obsessive-compulsive disorder when I was a player. Everything about my uniform, I was concerned about, down to the tape on my hands.

I'd actually hold my arms up to the mirror, and if they weren't even, I'd get 'em that way. My thumbs had to be taped exactly the same way, my socks had to be pulled up the same height and the stripes in the same spot.

I would even stress out during the game if I sweated so much the tape would start coming loose. If that happened and we lost the game, I'd be in the locker room going, "That fucking tape came loose and we lost the game."

IT'S MILLEN TIME

You might not expect Matt Millen—former TV guy, now the Lions' general manager, looks comfortable in a suit—to be much like me.

But we both played defense, and I liked him. I respected him because we were kind of in the same vein as players, with the sarcastic sense of humor.

We played the Raiders this one time, there was a TV timeout when he was on the sideline and I was on the field. Man, I hated those things, waiting around for ages during a commercial—that's when you'd get the coldest in one of those frozen games we were always playing.

When you're playing the Raiders, invariably during a TV timeout there's going to be a wisecrack coming from somewhere.

This particular game, we beat them 6-0 in Los Angeles. Millen's about the same size as me, and Hampton and Dent always called me the midget. I'm sure he got that from his team, too.

Anyway, I heard him call out, "McMichael, you're so short I could eat pea soup off of your head." I looked back at him, and Tom Flores and Al Davis, the coach and the owner, were standing there. I cracked his whole team up with my retort:

"Millen, I've seen longer legs on a coffee table."

MONGOISM #3

If you practice full speed, you know the speed of the game. If someone tells you the big adjustment for him is the speed of the pro game, he's practicing half-assed.

COVERT OPERATIONS

Jim Covert had the best technique at run blocking I've ever gone against. Most guys make the mistake of trying to get their head and body into you at the same time as their hands. That's compact. You can get around that. Jimbo led with his hands first to grab you. There was going to be contact, but his hands were on you straight up out of his stance before the body contact.

WORLD TRAVELERS

Because we were such a big draw after winning our Super Bowl, the league was always sending us to play in those American Bowls, preseason games in Europe. The first one was in '86, when we played the Cowboys in London, and our last one was against the 49ers in Berlin in '91. In between, we played the Vikings in Sweden—kind of appropriate, don't you think?

Europeans may not have known American football very well, but they did appreciate the contact. Every time there was a big hit, there'd be a big roar—well, with one notable exception in Sweden.

Right out of the box, Kevin Butler should have known Sweden wasn't for him. First night there, we had a drink with Ditka in the hotel lobby. Maybe more than one drink. We were relaxing. Butler got so drunk, he just leaned over and threw up right on the hotel lobby floor, right in front of the coach.

He was out of it. I had to pick him up, take him back to his room and throw him on his bed. So I did that, then I ripped his shirt open, poured baby powder all over his chest and stomach and wrote "pussy" in the powder. There's still a picture of that floating around somewhere.

That wasn't Kevin's lowlight of the trip, though.

The hotel had a little outdoor bistro—you know, al fresco dining—and Kevin and I and our wives were sitting at a table having something to eat. This bum walked by on the sidewalk, stopped at our table, leaned over, and we didn't understand what he was saying, because he was talking in Swedish. Finally, I guess he got frustrated, and he spit on the table. Butler stood up and hit him right in the face with a nice jab. Bam! Knocked the guy down. Well, Kevin got scared because we weren't in America. He ran up in the hotel. He shouldn't have worried, because the bum got up and walked off—actually, I was kind of disappointed he couldn't knock the guy out. Anyway, I went up to try to find Kevin, and when I got to his floor, he was hiding behind a plant in the elevator lobby. I was laughing my ass off so hard I could barely tell him he was off the hook.

MONGOISM #4

Guys come up to me to this day and say, "I was going to play pro ball, but I hurt my knee." Look, pal, I had eight knee operations and that didn't stop me.

MUSCLE VS. BULK

When I played, I was listed at 6'2", 268 pounds. That would just about make me a linebacker today. My heaviest was 284, and I always had a waist. Seems like every tackle in the league is at least 300 pounds, and Ted Washington, who went to the Pro Bowl with the Bears in 2002, was pushing 400.

Put it this way—Fridge, at 305, used to be an anomaly. Now he'd be undersized.

I think it's stupid. Now, you've got situational pass rushers—little, fast guys who aren't that strong—and big fatasses to stop the run.

I took care of both of those. I didn't weigh a ton, so I was fast enough to get to the quarterback. But I got in the weight room and made my ass strong, too, so I could handle the run.

SEEING THROUGH THE HAZE

One of the reasons I got "Ming the Merciless" was because I was so merciless breaking down a guy's weakest point with my sarcastic humor. "Boy, you got your ass toasted that time, didn't you, pal?"

I could tell other guys were thinking, "Why'd you say that, you insensitive so-and-so?" I didn't care how sensitive a guy was. Get him over that, he becomes a player.

Most rookies in training camp, you'd have the rookie show, make 'em get up on stage.

The big thing about that was how we reacted. It wouldn't be hazing them. It'd be ignoring them. We'd walk by without acknowledging they were standing there.

They'd be like little puppies, looking for affection, for acceptance. Our thinking was if they couldn't get it that way, they'd try to get it by busting their asses on the football field. Then you'd go, "Atta boy."

MONGOISM #5

I don't care how much you try to deny it or hide it, it's always in there festering—the defense hates the offense and the offense hates the defense. Can't help it; we're all just brainwashed that way.

GAPS IN THE STORY

I think a lot of old athletes are like me in one respect.

Sometimes it's hard to remember details—not because we got hit on the head too many times, but because of the way we had to approach our jobs.

The worst thing about it is family and friends got neglected because of this. It sounds chicken shit, but in my mind I had to do it to get where I did, I had to put the blinders on and focus

Being retired from football has allowed me to spend more time with my wife, Misty. (Don Rogers Photography, Austin)

on what was in front of me, not what was off to the sides. I probably had to do it because of the negative the Patriots had planted in my mind in the first place. I needed the blinders, the concentration, to get it done.

My family and friends missed out on a lot of me—because I was neglecting them for that focus.

Friday night, Saturday in particular, they'd come in for the game. Well, I didn't have time for them. It's the day before the game, you know?

There have been bad feelings, and I resent myself for it, but it's what I had to do.

WHAT BRIAN LACKS

I always hear people saying Brian Urlacher, the new darling of Bears fans, can't take on a block. I say he doesn't spend enough time in the weight room to be strong enough to take on a block.

In my estimation, you should be the one striking the blow on the offensive lineman. He's standing there letting the blow come to him instead of taking it to the blocker.

MONGOISM #6

Football is fun. The job part is getting ready to play four or five hours a day in the weight room. You better work harder to get your ass ready to play than you actually play on the field. Then the games are easy.

There's an equation for you: Practice hard, easy game.